MODERN
NATIONS
—OF THE—
WORLD

CAMBODIA

TITLES IN THE MODERN NATIONS OF THE WORLD SERIES INCLUDE:

Afghanistan	Jordan
Australia	Kenya
Austria	Lebanon
Brazil	Mexico
Cambodia	Nigeria
Canada	Norway
China	Pakistan
Cuba	Peru
Czech Republic	Poland
England	Russia
Ethiopia	Saudi Arabia
France	Scotland
Germany	Somalia
Greece	South Africa
Haiti	South Korea
Hungary	Spain
India	Sweden
Iran	Switzerland
Iraq	Taiwan
Ireland	Thailand
Israel	Turkey
Italy	United States
Japan	Vietnam

MODERN
NATIONS
—OF THE—
WORLD

CAMBODIA

BY ROBERT GREEN

LUCENT
BOOKS®

San Diego • Detroit • New York • San Francisco • Cleveland
New Haven, Conn. • Waterville, Maine • London • Munich

THOMSON
★ ™
GALE

On cover: A group of children travels by elephant through the streets of Phnom Penh.

LIBRARY OF CONGRESS CATALOGING-IN-PUBLICATION DATA

Green, Robert
   Cambodia / by Robert Green.
p. cm. — (Modern nations of the world)
Includes bibliographical references and index.
Summary: Discusses the physical topography, people, governments, culture, history, and future of Cambodia.
  ISBN 1-59018-109-3 (hardback : alk. paper)
  1. Cambodia—Juvenile Literature. I. Title. II. Series
  DS554.3 .G7 2003
  959.6—dc21

           2002011294

Printed in the United States of America

CONTENTS

INTRODUCTION

THE CIVILIZATION OF THE KHMER

Northeast of the Tonle Sap, the Grand Lac, or Great Lake of Cambodia, five stone towers shaped like lotus buds rise from the surrounding jungle. This is the temple of Angkor Wat, the world's largest religious complex. It faces west, where the sun drops daily over the horizon, plunging the land into darkness.

Angkor Wat has survived the destruction of invading armies and the madness of Cambodia's civil war. It is one of the most stunning archaeological sites on earth and a testament to the genius of its Khmer builders. The Khmer, the main ethnic group of Cambodia, constructed Angkor Wat as the main temple of Angkor, the capital city of Cambodia from the ninth to the fifteenth century.

To reach the present-day capital of Cambodia, Phnom Penh, from Angkor, boats ply the Tonle Sap southward along the Sap River, until it empties into the Mekong River. The Mekong slices Cambodia from north to south before spilling into the South China Sea. The Mekong and the Tonle Sap are the two great waterways of Cambodia. Their waters provide fish for food, irrigation for crops, and a highway for boats.

Because Cambodia's borders are relatively easy to cross, for most of its history Cambodia has had contact with its neighbors. At its height, the Khmer civilization of Angkor spilled over into Thailand and Laos. Invaders, in turn, poured over the border hills and sacked the great city. At one time or another, Cambodia has been invaded and occupied by the Thai, the French, and the Vietnamese.

THE KILLING FIELDS

The invader that wrought the most destruction on Cambodia, however, was not an army; it was an idea. That idea was communism, a revolutionary political ideology that originated in Europe during the nineteenth century and took root in Asia in the midtwentieth century. Two of Cambodia's neighbors, Laos and Vietnam, as well as China, the largest and most populous country in Asia, adopted Communist governments, and all three countries are to this day ruled by political parties that describe themselves as Communist.

Cambodia's version of communism sprang largely from the mind of the son of a well-to-do farmer. He was born Saloth Sar, but is known to the world as Pol Pot. As a youth, Pol Pot spent time with leftists in Paris and Yugoslavia. Like many future Asian Communist leaders, Pol Pot was greatly influenced by the radical ideas that were openly discussed and advocated in Western intellectual circles. And when he returned to Cambodia, he became a leading figure in the Cambodian Communist Party.

The king of Cambodia dubbed the Communists the Khmer Rouge, which means the "Red Khmer" in French, the

Angkor Wat is the world's largest religious complex, and its temples are testaments to the architectural genius of the Khmer civilization.

language of colonial Cambodia. The Communists wanted to rid Cambodia not only of the French, who had ruled Cambodia as a colony since 1863, but also of the king, whom they viewed as an oppressor of the common people.

Pol Pot led the insurrection from secret guerilla bases in the jungle, and slowly won support for his revolution among the rural people of Cambodia. When the victorious Khmer Rouge marched into Phnom Penh in 1975, they declared a brave new beginning for Cambodia, with Pol Pot as dictator.

In Year Zero of the revolution, as Pol Pot declared the first year of his reign, he emptied the cities of Cambodia. Professionals, the educated, and those who simply did not want to leave were murdered. The rest were forced to work on farms, and many died in the vast killing fields of the countryside for offenses such as wearing glasses or speaking French. Pol Pot and his men also killed Buddhists, ethnic minorities, and anyone who resisted his scheme to remake Cambodian

A museum exhibit of human skulls teaches Cambodian children about the brutality of the Khmer Rouge regime.

society into an agrarian utopia. During the five years that the Khmer Rouge ruled Cambodia, one in seven Cambodians perished. The rule of Pol Pot ended only when the Vietnamese army invaded in 1979.

A NATION ON THE MEND

Today, Cambodia is at peace. The nation is ruled by a coalition government voted into power in UN-monitored elections in 1993. The streets of Phnom Penh, eerily silent under the Khmer Rouge, now hum with life. Cafés serve French bread and coffee to those with a taste for the traditional French cuisine that still survives in modern Cambodia. Street vendors sell all manner of pungent spices and tropical fruits grown in the lush forests of Cambodia. And young people on scooters weave through crowds of shoppers, Buddhist monks, and the tourists who have started to return to Cambodia.

But the struggle for peace in Cambodia has just begun. Reminders of the war years are all around. In Phnom Penh monuments to the dead are prominent, while in the countryside bright signs with skull-and-crossbones symbols warn of unexploded mines. Sappers proceed slowly with the dangerous job of defusing the unexploded bombs and live mines left from years of war, but the number of people with missing limbs is a gruesome reminder of the danger that lies beneath the soil in many parts of Cambodia.

Today, Cambodia's government is an uneasy coalition. Prime Minister Hun Sen who was himself a member of the Khmer Rouge, has emerged as a strongman capable of ruthless tactics. His government struggles to restore public trust and mend a nation ravaged by war.

Meanwhile, a ferocious debate rages over the fate of surviving Khmer Rouge leaders. Pol Pot escaped justice by dying in the jungle in 1998, but many others move freely in Cambodia. The government has so far rejected UN proposals for international trials, arguing that Cambodia's problems are best handled by Cambodians. Though the problems of rebuilding their nation after years of war and five years of genocide are complex, Cambodians are now freer than ever to decide their own future.

1

THE LAND

Cambodia has been both blessed and cursed by its geography. The land itself is rich—the soil is fertile and water for irrigation is plentiful. Resources such as timber and rubber are easily harvested and in great supply. Cambodia's lakes and rivers abound with fish, and fruit grows in abundance. This Eden, however, is cursed in that its natural boundaries are easy to cross. Although Cambodia is bordered by highlands on three sides and the sea on the fourth, none of these boundaries present much of an obstacle to the invader. Cambodia's history and culture have been greatly shaped by this accessibility. Because Cambodia's neighbors have played such an influential role in shaping Cambodian history, Cambodia must be examined as a part of Southeast Asia.

Southeast Asia droops from the great landmass of East Asia like the floppy ear of an elephant. Cambodia is nestled in the middle of that elephant ear, bordered by Thailand to the west and north, Laos to the north, and Vietnam to the east and south. Cambodia is spared from being landlocked, like its northern neighbor Laos, by a stretch of sea along its southwestern border. But even the name of that sea—the Gulf of Thailand—reminds the Cambodians of the presence of their powerful neighbor to the west.

Cambodia was one of three countries ruled by France as Indochina, the French name for the eastern part of Southeast Asia, comprising the present-day countries of Cambodia, Vietnam, and Laos. With an area of about 69,000 square miles (about 180,000 square kilometers), Cambodia is the smallest of the former French colonies in Indochina. It is almost twice the size of Portugal and slightly smaller than the American state of Oklahoma. If Cambodia were in the Western hemisphere, it would fall about where the Central American countries of Nicaragua and Costa Rica are located, centered about 12 degrees north of the equator.

TOPOGRAPHY

Cambodia's topography is distinguished by stretches of flatlands interrupted by sloping hills, known as *phnoms* in Khmer, the principal language of Cambodia. The exception to this rolling countryside are the mountain ranges along Cambodia's border regions.

Along the southwestern border, where Cambodia opens onto the Gulf of Thailand, the flat plains of central Cambodia rise into two mountain ranges: the Cardamom and Elephant ranges. The Cardamom is the higher of the two ranges and includes Cambodia's highest peak, Phnom Aural, which rises to a height of 5,937 feet (1,810 meters). Along these mountain chains grow tropical forests and at the highest reaches pine groves. The forests of these highlands are a rich source of timber for Cambodia.

In the northern part of the country, the land again rises, into the Dangrek Mountains, which run along Cambodia's border with Thailand. In the eastern part of Cambodia, the land rises

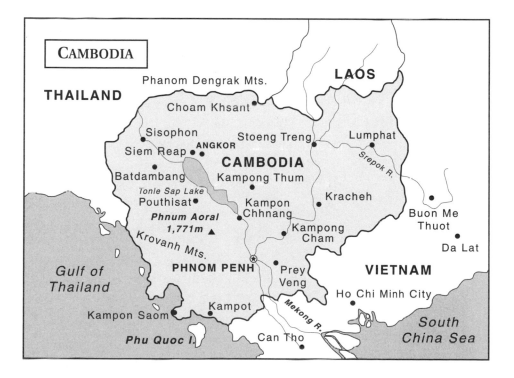

into a high plateau that runs across the border into Vietnam. This plateau is carpeted with tall grasses and sporadic forests.

If mountains and highlands are the most salient features of Cambodia's border regions, the center of the country is dominated by two great water systems. The first of these is the Mekong River. The Mekong River traverses Cambodia from north to south for about three hundred miles (five hundred kilometers). At more than two thousand miles in total length, the Mekong is the world's tenth-longest river. It originates in the mountains of western China and runs southward, ever in search of lower ground, through Laos, Cambodia, and Vietnam until it splits into the many rivulets of the Mekong Delta in Southern Vietnam. The rivulets of the Mekong Delta in turn spill into the South China Sea.

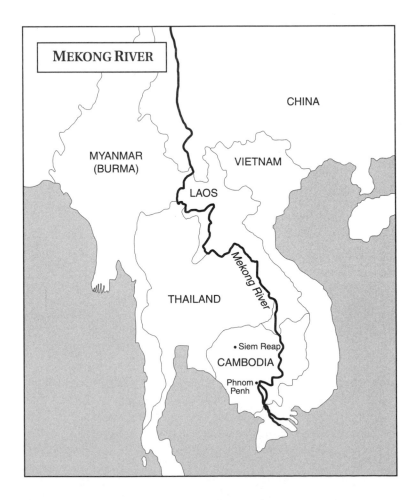

WHAT'S IN A NAME?

Cambodia has been known by many names. The word *Cambodia* is derived from "Kambujadesha" or "Kambuja," "the land of Kambu," the Hindu god who is also the mythical father of the Cambodians, according to Hindu legend. The name is evidence of the Indian influence on the Khmer civilization. Today, Hinduism has faded along with other Indianized aspects of Cambodian life, but the name Cambodia remains.

In more recent times, Cambodia's official name has shifted with the political identity of the nation. In 1953, when Cambodia proclaimed its independence from the French, the formal name Kingdom of Cambodia was inaugurated. When King Sihanouk was overthrown in 1970, the name changed to the Khmer Republic. Under Pol Pot, the country was Democratic Kampuchea. Under Vietnamese rule, it was called the People's Republic of Kampuchea. After the Vietnamese withdrew, Cambodia became the State of Cambodia. And after the elections of 1993, when the monarchy regained official status in Cambodia, the country once again became the Kingdom of Cambodia.

The Mekong is the greatest water system of Southeast Asia. As the primary waterway from China through all the countries once known as Indochina, it has anchored the great civilizations of Southeast Asia. The peoples of Laos, Cambodia, and Vietnam still rely on the Mekong as a transportation artery, as a primary source of irrigation for crops, and as a rich ground for fishing.

THE TONLE SAP

In Cambodia, the Mekong has a rival. The Sap River sprouts from the Tonle Sap, or Great Lake, located in northwestern Cambodia. The Sap River, actually a tributary of the Mekong, provides Cambodia with a second major waterway. The waters of the Sap River empty, for at least part of the year, into the Mekong River at the spot where Phnom Penh, the Cambodian capital, was constructed.

The Sap River annually performs a feat that is as remarkable as it is rare for a river: It changes direction. This is moody behavior for a river on which so many people depend. The change of direction, however, is performed neither by the command of the all-powerful Hindu god Shiva—long worshiped in Cambodia—nor at the whim of the Buddhist gods that are revered in Cambodia today. It is the result of the Sap River's relationship with the Mekong.

From mid-May to October, when the skies open over Cambodia and monsoon rains soak the earth, the Mekong rises to the point that its waters run into the Sap River basin. This reverses the flow of the Sap River from south to north and causes Sap River waters to empty into the Tonle Sap instead of flowing out of it. The influx of water causes the Tonle Sap to swell dramatically. During the wet season it covers nearly a seventh of Cambodia's surface. During the dry months, the waters of the Mekong fall and the Sap River again turns toward the south and drains into the Mekong.

The Tonle Sap acts as a sponge, holding much of Cambodia's valuable rainwater for the drier months, when it is slowly released into the Sap River. As it releases its stored up water, the Great Lake shrinks to a quarter of its rainy-season size. At its height, the Tonle Sap is 45 feet (14 meters) deep; during the dry months, it falls to an average of 6 ½ feet (2 meters).

As this great freshwater lake recedes during Cambodia's dry months, organic matter is concentrated in the shrinking remainder of the lake. The lake becomes a giant feeding ground for fish, who sup off the nutrient-rich matter in the lake. Fish plucked from the waters of the Tonle Sap, the Sap River, and the Mekong provide Cambodians with one of the staples of the Cambodian diet.

The most common crop of Cambodia's farms is rice, and the life-giving Tonle Sap plays a part in enriching the rice paddies near its shores. When the Tonle Sap shrinks during the dry season, it deposits a dark, loamy soil on the surrounding fields. This soil fertilizes the local farms as its waters irrigate the fields.

In short, the Tonle Sap provides an entire support system for the people of northwestern Cambodia. To see the standing oarsmen pilot their tiny boats across the surface of the Tonle Sap or the turbaned farmers harvest rice from the green paddies by its shores is to witness the intimate connection between the people of Cambodia and the Tonle Sap.

CLIMATE

The rains that swell the Mekong and Sap Rivers are the result of the distinguishing feature of Southeast Asia's climate —the monsoon. There are two monsoon seasons in Cambodia. The wetter of the two monsoons hits Cambodia from the southwest from May to October, bringing torrential rainfall and culminating in the wettest months of September and October.

Average rainfall in the central plains of Cambodia is about 55 inches (1.4 meters) per year, but the slopes of the southern mountains that face the sea and catch the brunt of the monsoons can receive 200 inches (5 meters) of rain per year. During the rainy season, many villages in Cambodia become islands floating in lakes of monsoon water. Land routes to these villages are often flooded for months at a time. For transportation the villagers rely on light boats or simply walk across the soaking soil through knee-deep water.

Between November and March the second monsoon arrives from the northeast, delivering slightly less rain than the southwest monsoon and bringing cooler air, which is a relief in one of the hottest countries of an extremely hot region. During the hottest months of the year, temperatures in Cambodia average 95°F and climb to 105°F. Even when the cooler winds of the northwest monsoon blow, temperatures rarely drop below 68° F (20° C).

RESOURCES

Its wet climate makes Cambodia ideal for cultivating crops, while its topography is ideal for human habitation. The central lowlands of Cambodia are fertile and well watered by river systems. Since earliest times, rice has been the main crop in Cambodia. Its importance to the Cambodian diet is evident in the Khmer verb "to eat," which can be translated literally as "to eat rice."

Rice is a crop that requires a great deal of water. Between the monsoons and the river systems, water is abundant in Cambodia. Cambodians plant rice seedlings in beds and allow them to sprout before transplanting them in the watery beds of the rice paddy.

The land must be flat to retain the water lying in the paddies, and Cambodia has many flat stretches throughout the country. Where the land is not naturally flat, it has

THE MAN-MADE LAKES OF CAMBODIA

The monsoons that drench Cambodia provide ample water for agriculture. However, the rain falls in concentrated periods. As the monsoons pass, the crops grow thirsty again. To water the crops during the dry season, Cambodians during the Angkor period developed a complex system of water tanks and irrigation channels to carry the water to the fields. The giant water reservoirs, called *barays*, collected rainwater and were often fed by nearby rivers. At Angkor, three main *barays*—the western, eastern, and the baray of Preah Khan—formed giant man-made lakes around the capital. A complicated system of channels provided water for the residents of the capital and irrigation for the fields in the surrounding countryside.

The kings of Angkor exercised power by controlling the water flow from the barays during the dry season, ensuring the importance of the capital city in the life of the surrounding villagers. The value of these man-made lakes to the rulers of Angkor can be seen in the fact that they built temples to the gods on tiny islands in the center of the reservoirs.

The baray *pictured here is one of three reservoirs the Khmer built around Angkor.*

been terraced to make flat steps along sloping hills, each of which supports a rice paddy. The sight of a terraced hill for the cultivation of rice is perhaps one of the most charming in Asia. The land is so subtly terraced that not until a person is fairly close does it become apparent that humans have reshaped the very surface of the hills.

A Chinese visitor to Cambodia in the late thirteenth century recorded even in that early period that Cambodians could rely on three or four rice crops a year. "There is, moreover, a certain kind of land where the rice grows natural, without sowing," wrote Zhou Daguan, the Chinese chronicler. "When the water is up one fathom, the rice keeps pace in its growth. This, I think, must be a special variety."[1] What the Chinese visitor had noticed was the fertility of Cambodia, on which its largely agricultural society and economy has been based to the present day.

Today Cambodia produces enough rice to sell a surplus on the open market. In the twentieth century, however, Cambodia has suffered famine repeatedly. The problem has been entirely created by humans, however, not natural forces. The Khmer Rouge, for example, attempted land reforms that actually decreased rice production because of poor organization. For much of the latter half of the twentieth century, Cambodians were unable to continue rice production because they were fleeing war zones. The constant flow of refugees left the rice paddies unattended and further intensified the suffering of Cambodians. Today, rice is once again a major export crop, notably to other Asian nations whose demand for rice is high but whose own rice crops are insufficient to feed their people.

Cambodia has also become an exporter of hardwood timber harvested from the highland regions of the north, west, and east. There, hardwood forests are being cleared for both domestic construction and exportation. The splendid stone monuments that dot the Cambodian landscape are the exception in Khmer building. Historically most Cambodian buildings, even at the time of the Angkor empire from the tenth to the thirteenth century, were made of wood. Today, wood is still the main building material, though concrete and steel are slowly replacing wood in the cities. In the countryside, much of which is flooded for part of the year, houses are often constructed on wooden stilts that elevate the dwelling above water level.

In earlier times, logging was carried out on a small scale and presented little environmental risk. In modern times, however, Cambodians and foreign investors alike have realized the export value of the treasured hardwood forests. Wood products fetch high prices in such places as Japan, where chopsticks and other wooden objects are used daily but domestic forests are limited. Modern methods of clear-cutting—the felling of huge swaths of forest at a time—are leading to environmental changes in Cambodia. Most significantly, clear-cutting often leads to flooding and soil erosion. Where once soil was firmly anchored by tree roots, now topsoil is washed away, taking nutrients with it.

Because of its relatively small population and limited industrial base, Cambodia does not yet face the pollution problems of many other Southeast Asian countries. Nevertheless, a country that relies on farming for its livelihood must grapple with the consequences of changing the environment for short-term payoffs. Compared with most industrialized nations, though, Cambodians have not had a major negative impact on their natural environment. One example is the degree to which Cambodians accept the creatures of the forests as their neighbors. Cambodia is a land rich in wildlife, and it is not uncommon to see an elephant sauntering down a country lane with a child *mahout*, or handler, perched on top. Monkeys can also be riotous companions on visits to temples and archaeological sites.

CREATURES OF THE JUNGLE

When French colonists stumbled upon the ruins of Angkor and other sites, they were presented with a remarkable vision. The sandstone pillars and crumbling stones presented an aura of mystery. The jungle growth crept up and into the temples, nearly hiding them from sight. The roots of banyan trees wrapped themselves around stone structures, a phenomenon which can still be seen at Angkor. To add to the general atmosphere of the lost jungle city, snakes slithered through the brush. Monkeys swung through the canopy of the forest chattering and screeching. And the racket of an elephant rustling through the dense foliage sent birds into flight.

Cambodia is a land teeming with wildlife. The tropical forests and abundant rainfall provide habitats for some of the earth's most extraordinary animals. The largest of Cambodia's creatures is the Asian elephant, which is slightly smaller and has smaller ears than its African counterpart. Cambodians have a long history of training elephants; ancient temple carvings depict kings and generals riding on these giant animals in regal celebrations and into battle.

Cambodians have become famous throughout the region for their skill in training and handling elephants. Even in Thailand, where the elephant is also common, Cambodian mahouts are often recruited for their expertise. A mahout often raises an elephant from birth and lives closely with the elephant for many years. Some elephants will refuse to be ridden by anyone other than their trusted mahout.

The ruins of Angkor Wat provide habitat for a wide variety of jungle plants and animals.

THE IRRAWADDY DOLPHIN

Of all the animal species native to Cambodia, the Irrawaddy dolphin is one of the rarest and most unusual. This playful creature can be seen leaping from the water, especially on the stretches of the Mekong above the town of Kratie, which is located north of Phnom Penh about halfway to Laos. This stretch of the Mekong all the way into Laos is home to an estimated 150 Irrawaddy dolphins.

These aquatic mammals grow six to ten feet in length and lack the long snout of more common species of ocean dolphins. These freshwater dolphins have heads shaped like a thumb, with round black eyes punctuating their blue-gray skins, and a mouth that makes them look like they are smiling.

During the Khmer Rouge regime, the dolphins fared no better than most Cambodians. They were killed wherever they were discovered, either with explosive charges or fishing nets. The dolphins have always been hunted for their meat and oil, but in recent years the government of Cambodia has sought to protect this rare creature.

Irrawaddy dolphin fins are displayed for sale at a Cambodian market.

Roaming the same stretches of jungle as the elephant are tigers, leopards, rhinoceroses, bears, and various species of deer. Bird and fish species are just as varied and plentiful. The fact that most Cambodians are Buddhists, who refrain from killing animals, allows a remarkable degree of coexistence between Cambodians and the varied wildlife of the country. It is not uncommon for wild animals to wander through Cambodian villages. Animals that are not threatening are often accepted as part of local life. Monkeys, for example, are often tolerated and even adopted by children as pets. When they begin to steal the laundry, however, they are often chased away.

The Buddhist precept that prohibits killing living creatures, even the smallest insects, is a factor in the acceptance of animals in the daily life of Cambodians. However, not all Cambodians are vegetarians. Today, Buddhists often rely on non-Buddhist ethnic minorities to catch their fish and slaughter animals for their dinner tables. This is just one of the roles that Cambodia's minority peoples have played in the culture of Cambodia.

THE KHMER AND
THEIR COMPATRIOTS

The principal people of Cambodia, the Khmer, are thought to be one of the most ancient peoples of Southeast Asia. Their origins are unclear, however, though archaeologists, interrupted by years of occupation and civil war, are once again excavating sites of early Khmer civilization. Part of the difficulty in tracing the origin of the Khmer is that their language was not written down until they adopted Sanskrit from India and modified it to suit their own spoken language. Another problem presented to archaeologists is that Khmer builders often used wood, which disintegrates over time in the humid atmosphere of Cambodia.

Nevertheless, the people of modern Cambodia are primarily Khmer. They are accompanied, however, by a diverse group of minority peoples. The relationship between the Khmer and these minorities has often been tense, reflecting the strained relationship between Cambodia and its neighbors, whence many of the minorities originate. In contemporary Cambodia, the Khmer and Cambodia's minority groups live together more or less peacefully. General peace in the region has helped smooth relations among Cambodia's various peoples.

THE KHMER

According to a Cambodian legend, the Hindu god Shiva arranged the marriage of Kambu, a hermit, and Mera, a beautiful nymph, and their offspring were the Khmer, the main ethnic group of Cambodia. The word *Khmer* is itself said to be the combination of the names Kambu and Mera.

The Khmer are one of the earliest groups of people to settle in Southeast Asia in great numbers. They originated in the southern mountains of China and migrated along the waterways of the great Mekong River, southward through Laos and into Cambodia. Evidence of their migration pattern is still visible in Laos, where communities of Khmer make up 15 to 20 percent of the population. The lower Mekong in southern Vietnam represents the end of the journey for the Khmer migrants. They settled in the rich alluvial plains of the Mekong Delta and today form a distinct ethnic minority in southern Vietnam. Cambodians call their kin in Vietnam the Khmer Krom, or "Lower Khmer."

It is in Cambodia, however, that the majority of the Khmer settled, and where their civilization flourished. The Cambodian government estimates that the Khmer constitute 96 percent of the population of Cambodia, a total of about 12.5 million. This percentage is thought to be inflated, however—a function of Khmer nationalism and an attempt to minimize the number of minority peoples. Although exact figures are unknown, most estimates indicate that the Khmer constitute at least 90 percent of the population of Cambodia. Even this revised figure clearly shows that in population Cambodia is the most homogeneous of all the states of Southeast Asia.

The Khmer are predominantly an agricultural people, and in Cambodia they have found a land well suited to

Most Khmer earn their livelihood from agriculture. Here, a family of farmers harvests rice in a paddy.

farming. Compared with the other countries of Southeast Asia, Cambodia has a low population density. Whereas their neighbors in mountainous Vietnam have had to terrace the hills to accommodate the essential rice paddy, the Cambodians were fortunate to have a relatively flat land with rich soil and plenty of water for irrigation. The Khmer, who have long been masters of irrigation techniques, today water their fields and grow rice much as they have done for centuries.

THE VIETNAMESE

Just as there are ethnic Khmer in Vietnam, there are ethnic Vietnamese in Cambodia. Estimates of their number vary widely. The government estimate, which routinely underestimates the number of Vietnamese in Cambodia, was one hundred thousand in 1995. Other sources estimate a Vietnamese population of five hundred thousand up to 1 million. The Cambodian government refers to the country's largest minority group as the Viet Kieu—migrant Vietnamese. The term underscores the lack of warmth that the Cambodians have traditionally expressed for the Vietnamese. Although in most cases the Vietnamese and Cambodians live together peacefully, their identities remain distinct and animosity sometimes rises to the surface.

The Vietnamese have tended to migrate to Cambodia from the south, where the Mekong River flows into Vietnam. The Mekong Delta is densely populated, and some Vietnamese have fled to Cambodia during times of crisis and in search of work. Historically, the tensions between the Khmer and the Vietnamese can be traced to the tug-of-war over the Mekong Delta, where the Khmer Krom were once dominant and still make up sizable communities. Some Cambodians see Vietnamese sovereignty over the Khmer Krom as an unnatural division of the Khmer people.

The Vietnamese in Cambodia today contribute to two main pillars of the economy—fishing and small business. Vietnamese fishermen from shoreline communities can be found up and down the Mekong and the Sap Rivers sinking their lines and casting their nets to haul up the rich variety of fish in Cambodia's rivers. Fish has become a staple of the

Cambodian diet because of its abundance, and many Vietnamese fishermen make a good living selling their catch.

Vietnamese in Cambodia who are not fishermen have tended to migrate to the cities. In Phnom Penh, Battambang, Kompong Cham, and other urban centers, ethnic Vietnamese have prospered as shopkeepers and small businessmen. Vietnamese restaurants have proven to be lucrative in the cities, where people tend to have more money to spend and less time to cook. The success of Vietnamese businessmen is often resented in Cambodia, adding another mark against the Vietnamese in the eyes of those already inclined to resent them. Despite the tension, the traditional occupations of the Vietnamese often contribute to the economy of Cambodia and to the diversity of its society.

THE CHINESE

The Chinese have been visiting Southeast Asia for at least as long as recorded history. The tremendous population of China led many Chinese to emigrate, setting up small communities throughout Asia, which came to serve as links in

Masked dragons entertain a Chinese girl during a Chinese New Year celebration in Phnom Penh. The Chinese play an influential role in Cambodia's economy.

a vast chain of Chinese commercial activity. Chinese merchants first arrived in Cambodia overland and by sea. Today, they come mainly by airplane, for the Chinese are still an active commercial force in Cambodia's economy.

It is estimated that between one hundred and four hundred thousand Chinese have made Cambodia their home. Like the Vietnamese, they have played a role in the urban life of Cambodia. Their extensive trading networks throughout Southeast Asia enabled them to import and export products. In many parts of Southeast Asia, the Chinese have developed distinct communities, with Chinese temples, restaurants, and business associations, that adhere to Chinese cultural traditions.

Business ties often depend on family or community ties back in China, and such connections link business transactions throughout Southeast Asia. For example, when a Chinese importer in Phnom Penh, whose family hails from Canton province in China, receives an order for Japanese-made CD players, he might relay the order to his relatives or kin in Guangzhou, the provincial capital of Canton. The two Chinese can speak in the southern Chinese dialect of Cantonese and trust each other because they are either related or have done business before.

Before the Khmer Rouge seized Cambodia in 1975, the Chinese and the Vietnamese competed for business in the cities along with Cambodians. Under the Khmer Rouge, however, minorities, including the Chinese and Vietnamese, were ruthlessly persecuted. As Cambodians were driven out of cities, many minorities were slaughtered immediately. More were executed over the years in the countryside and many died from disease or starvation.

Pol Pot, the leader of the Khmer Rouge, believed that non-Khmer had contributed to what he considered the decadent state of Cambodian society. He intended to rid Cambodia of all foreign influences. Many Vietnamese and Chinese fled Cambodia during the Khmer Rouge regime. The fortunate ones were taken in by relatives in other countries. Some ended up in refugee camps. One group who found it difficult to elude the murderous soldiers of the Khmer Rouge was one of the ancient peoples of Indochina—the Cham.

THE CHAM

The Cham are unrelated to the Khmer and other peoples of Southeast Asia who made their way southward from China. They came by sea routes and share a blood kinship with Malays and Indonesians. The physical features and dress of the Cham set them apart from their fellow Cambodians. They have the appearance of Austronesian peoples, who are of a slightly slimmer build than most Cambodians. Men and women often wear sarongs—a long cloth wound around the bottom half of the body like a skirt—similar to those worn by Malays. The Cham are also a distinct religious minority in Cambodia. In a country where Buddhism is dominant, the Cham are Muslims, adherents of Islam.

A Cham woman smiles for a photo. Distinct from other Cambodian ethnic groups, the Cham live in close-knit communities in remote villages.

Being a trading people and always somewhat apart from the Cambodians among whom they lived, the Cham adopted Islam from their contact with Muslim seafarers in the ports along Vietnam's coast. Unlike Buddhism, therefore, Islam arrived in Cambodia not by overland routes but through the maritime trading communities along the coasts of Southeast Asia.

But the Cham were not always Muslim. Islam arose in the deserts of western Arabia in the seventh century and made its way slowly to East Asia. The Cham predate the rise of Islam. As early as A.D. 192, Chinese documents record a Cham kingdom called Champa. The kingdom of Champa extended from mid-Vietnam, near the Vietnamese imperial capital at the city of Hue, southward to the Mekong Delta in southern Vietnam. Today, lonely brick towers can be seen rising from the earth in the central and southern provinces of Vietnam. These towers are the legacy of the Cham, who built them during the height of their empire. In

 ## THE BLUE MOSQUES OF THE CHAM

The Cham people of Cambodia witnessed in the years of the Khmer Rouge regime the destruction of their places of worship, known as mosques. Before the Khmer Rouge seized power in 1975, Cham mosques dotted the landscape in Phnom Penh, Battambang, Kampong Cham, and everywhere communities of Chams lived. The mosque is the center of religious life for Muslims, who are required by their religion to pray five times a day. In the Middle East, the call to prayer comes from a crier who calls the faithful to prayer in a melodious wail. In Cambodia the call to prayer reaches the ears in the form of a drumbeat.

The Cham are Sunni Muslims, the more populous of the two great sects of Islam. Since the fall of the Khmer Rouge regime, the Cham have rebuilt many mosques and restored those that survived. A unique feature of Cham mosques is the decorative use of blue paint. Traditionally, the color of Islam is green, but the Cham have expressed their beliefs in a manner that suits their own taste.

1471, the Vietnamese launched an assault on the Cham kingdom, greatly reducing its size. In 1720, the Cham empire collapsed altogether when their king refused to submit to the encroaching Vietnamese, choosing instead to flee northward along the Mekong River into Cambodia.

The Cham settled along the Mekong and Sap Rivers, where they still make a living by fishing, working as silversmiths, and butchering meat for Buddhists. The Cham are most numerous in the province of Kampong Cham, which bears their name.

When Pol Pot came to power in 1975, he tried to eradicate all influences and peoples that he believed were alien to Cambodia. The Cham were immediately chosen for extermination. The fact that they looked different from other Cambodians and practiced what Pol Pot considered a foreign religion marked them as obvious targets for the atheistic regime. Estimates indicate that one-half to two-thirds of Cambodia's entire population of about four hundred thousand Cham were victims of the Khmer Rouge. Some were killed outright, some fled the country, and others starved to death or died of disease. The Cham today enjoy the same rights as other Cambodians. They openly practice their Islamic beliefs, and their numbers are increasing again.

THE KHMER LOEU

One minority group that fared well under the Khmer Rouge was the Khmer Loeu, or Upland Khmer. They are so named because they live in the remote highlands of Cambodia. Their population is estimated at about sixty thousand to seventy thousand, and they live in communities mainly in the provinces of Ratanakiri, Mondulkiri, Stung Treng, and Kratie. The largest group, the Tapuon, number about fifteen thousand.

The Khmer Loeu make their living by hunting, gathering, and small-scale farming. Historically, the Khmer have tended to look down on these more primitive people, who are largely illiterate and unfamiliar with modern technology and modern devices. The Khmer Rouge, however, admired the Khmer Loeu's lack of familiarity with the modern world. Pol Pot's dream was to return Cambodia to an earlier state of subsistence farming. The city was considered a breeding ground for corruption and evil. Learning was scorned and distrusted. The Khmer Rouge found in the Khmer Loeu a model for their ideal citizen. As a result, the were generally spared the harsh treatment received by other minorities in Cambodia under Pol Pot's regime. In fact, they found themselves held up as an example of the ideal Cambodian, living off the land and untainted by the modern world or outside ideas.

Khmer Rouge leaders also found that the Khmer Loeu were largely docile and compliant people, not inclined to rebellion. Their loyalty and obedience made them ideal bodyguards for Khmer Rouge leaders. In the early days of the Khmer Rouge regime, when internal power struggles broke out, the Khmer Loeu provided a secure force of bodyguards for leaders who feared betrayal by ambitious rivals. Khmer Loeu women were especially favored as bodyguards, and some commanders, such as the feared, one-legged Ta Mok, were surrounded only by female bodyguards of the Khmer Loeu.

THE LANGUAGES OF CAMBODIA

The Khmer Loeu also speak their own languages. These languages are related to Khmer, and sometimes are mixed with Khmer to varying degrees. Linguists categorize Khmer and the languages of the hill people under the Mon-Khmer language group, which is a subset of the Austro-Asiatic group of languages spoken throughout Southeast Asia. Khmer is the official language spoken by government officials and by upwards of 95 percent of the population. It is the native language of the Khmer people and the language formally taught in Cambodian schools.

Mon-Khmer is thought to be one of the oldest language groups of Southeast Asia because of the high number of dialects and the far-flung nature of the remote communities that still speak those dialects. In other words, it took a very long time for Mon Khmer dialects to evolve, die out, and be preserved in relatively isolated pockets. There are Mon-Khmer speakers in Thailand, Laos, Vietnam, Myanmar (Burma), and Malaysia. In Cambodia, the diversity of the Mon-Khmer lan-

DISPLACED PERSONS

The Khmer Rouge policies of emptying the cities and forcing Cambodians to relocate to the countryside caused a wholesale shift in the population of the country. Cities were vacated and entire villages moved or destroyed entirely. As the severity of the life under Pol Pot's new society became clear, many Cambodians fled the country. The most common route of escape was to Thailand, where refugee camps were set up to hold the fleeing Cambodians.

Joan Criddle and Teeda Butt Mam relate in their book *To Destroy You Is No Loss* the harrowing journey of Teeda's escape into Thailand: "We waded through leech- and snake-infested waters up to our necks, carrying Mum and the children on our shoulders." Teeda survived four years of forced labor in the fields of Cambodia before reaching safety in Thailand at age twenty. Today, she lives in the United States, but more than 370,000 refugees have returned to Cambodia since 1992, when the United Nations began repatriating Cambodians from refugee camps in Thailand and elsewhere.

guage group can be seen in the diversity of the dialects spoken among the hill tribes.

Unlike Chinese and Vietnamese, Khmer is a nontonal language; that is, a word's meaning does not depend on the rising and falling sound of a syllable's pronunciation. Its grammar is fairly simple. Verbs, for example, are not conjugated and tense is indicated, if at all, by adding particles after the verb or at the end of the sentence. In spoken Khmer, the tense of a verb is generally determined by the situation. In other words, if in English one says, "He arrived yesterday," in Khmer the verb would be in an unconjugated form "arrive"—but the addition of the word "yesterday" would make it clear that the action happened in the past.

The richness of expression of Khmer is achieved more through the use of colorful and varied verbs and nouns than with adjectives or other modifiers. This gives the language a richness of imagery, since the verb, which conveys the action, is stressed. Khmer is also specific in its terms of address. Like Chinese, it has specific words to indicate the relationships between family members. Much of this is meant to reflect the respect that older or distinguished people are afforded in Cambodian society. For example, more formal terms of address are used when addressing elders, Buddhist monks, and others who hold a higher rank on the social scale.

THE WINDING PATH OF SANSKRIT

The written language of Cambodia is derived from the writing, known as Sanskrit, of the Hindu holy men and Indian merchants who arrived in Cambodia in the early Middle Ages. In the time of the Angkor civilization, Sanskrit was used as the court language. A Sanskrit inscription carved on one temple, for example, retells the history of Cambodia, interwoven with myths and legends from India and Hindu aphorisms. "The just man supports the Dharma [the basic principles of cosmic or individual existence], the unjust destroys it," reads one Sanskrit inscription, "but of the two the first is stronger."[2]

Sanskrit was slowly modified by Cambodians and adopted as the written form of Khmer, which was until then only spoken. Khmer is a phonetic language with an alphabet, meaning words can be sounded out by reading the sounds of letters in the order that they are written. It is unlike written Chinese, which is still used among Cambodia's Chinese community. The Chinese system is based on symbolic characters that must be memorized, though they contain some phonetic clues in their structure. The Cham, adherents of Islam, use Arabic writing, which Muslims believe to be the language of God, whom they call Allah. Because Arabic is considered to be sacred in itself, the holy book of Muslims, called the Koran, is almost always read in the original Arabic.

Like Arabic, Khmer is written from left to right. The language has a beautiful curving script form whose interpretation can pose a time-consuming challenge for a foreigner. To simplify translation, during the colonial era the French romanized Khmer script. The romanization system is complicated and has many irregularities, but it is an essential bridge to learning Khmer for foreigners. The legacy of French colonial rule is evident by the fact that some elderly Cambodians still speak the colonial language.

THE TURBAN OF CAMBODIA

One legacy of the Indianization of medieval Cambodia can still be seen in the form of a head scarf known as a *krama*. The *krama* is most often worn like a turban, headwear traditionally worn by Indian men. In Cambodia, the *krama* is worn by both men and women. Farmers working in the fields will often wear the *krama* as a headress to shade themselves from the sun. It is also worn around the neck as a scarf, tied around the waist like a sash, or draped like a sarong.

Cambodians are the only people of Southeast Asia to wear the *krama*, and the most popular pattern—the checked *krama*—is something of an unofficial national symbol of Cambodia. It also serves as an all-purpose carrier for Cambodians. Babies rest in the folds of *kramas* slung over their mothers' backs. Drivers of motorcycles might use the *krama* to secure their vegetables from the market as they speed off in a cloud of exhaust. Sometimes in the heat of the day, the *krama* will be suspended like a parasol to provide sanctuary from the beating midday sun. The *krama* is a testament to the whimsical ingenuity of the people of Cambodia.

Khmer soldiers wearing krama *scarves assemble for inspection.*

Modern Cambodia is the result of the blending of many influences. It is a great tribute to the Cambodian people that they could weave so many disparate elements into a particularly Cambodian civilization. Today, the different ethnic groups of Cambodia blend more harmoniously than they have in the past. Cambodia has in fact always been greatly impacted by outside influences, even during the age of Angkor, when Khmer civilization was at its zenith.

THE RISE AND FALL OF ANGKOR

In 1860, a Frenchman trekking through the jungle near the town of Siem Reap on the banks of the Tonle Sap came upon the splendid sight of the ancient city of Angkor. "There are ruins of such grandeur," wrote the Frenchman, Henri Mahout, "remains of structures that must have been raised at such an immense cost of labor that . . . one is filled with profound admiration, and cannot but ask what has become of this powerful race, so civilized, so enlightened, the authors of these gigantic works?"[3]

Henri Mahout was a naturalist and a citizen of France, the colonial power in the Southeast Asian countries of Vietnam and Laos. Just three years after Mahout recorded his impressions of Angkor, the French forced the king of Cambodia to become a vassal of the French and a part of French Indochina. The observations of Mahout describe the intersection of two worlds. The colonial Frenchman gazed with Western scientific curiosity at the abandoned ruins of the imperial capital of Angkor and asked what happened to that great civilization. "It is grander than anything left to us by Greece or Rome," he wrote, "and presents a sad contrast to the barbarism in which [Cambodia] is now plunged."[4]

The Frenchman could not credit the subject people of Cambodia with the architectural wonder he saw before him at Angkor. The French were frequently contemptuous of their colonial subjects. But those subjects, the Cambodians, had once been the great power of Southeast Asia, ruling an empire that stretched from Burma to Vietnam. From their capital at Angkor, the Khmer governed a civilization that was a rich blend of Indian philosophy and religion and Khmer ingenuity. Their builders took for inspiration the Hindu gods Shiva and Vishnu, and the teachings of Buddha, who was celebrated side by side with the god-kings of the pre-Angkorean tradition.

THE SERPENT-HEADED NAGA

One of the most common symbols found in Cambodia is also one of the most ancient. The cobra-headed *naga* adorns many buildings at Angkor and even pre-Angkorean sites. The *nagas* were fashioned from bronze or carved from sandstone. They are most common as decorations for the *barays*, or water reservoirs, that provided water for irrigation. The *naga* is in fact a water symbol, often portrayed with three separate cobra heads. The hoods of the three cobras usually run together to form one great hood. From the separate heads, the *naga* figures run down into a single snakelike body. These frightening symbols also acted as guardians for the prosperity of the kingdom and stood as a warning to those who wanted to steal from the god-kings of Cambodia.

CAMBODIA BEFORE ANGKOR

The historical record shows that at least four thousand years ago people were living in what is now Cambodia. Along the Mekong and Sap Rivers, communities lived by fishing and growing rice. There is evidence that they lived in houses built on stilts to accommodate the rivers' rising waters during the monsoon seasons. Stilt houses are still a common sight in Cambodia, where entire villages can be surrounded by water for many months of the year.

Records of an early Khmer state come from Chinese travelers who visited Southeast Asia on diplomatic and trading missions. The Chinese reported that a kingdom, which they called Funan, existed in the Mekong Delta region, where the Khmer Krom, or Lower Khmer, still live today. This kingdom was separate from the kingdom of Champa, which stretched from the delta region into central Vietnam.

The kingdom of Funan derived its wealth from trade along the coast. The traders who bought and sold their wares in Funan's ports were a link in an extensive trade route that ended as far west as Rome. Roman coins dating from the second century have been discovered in southern Vietnam at a place known as Oc-Eo, which might have been the capital of the kingdom of Funan and was certainly one of the larger trading centers of the region.

The Chinese also recorded that tribute was paid by the kingdom of Funan to China. This tribute generally guaranteed friendly relations with the Chinese Empire. Korea, Vietnam, and other vassal states paid tribute to the Chinese in recognition of China's greater military power. There is no record, however, of the Chinese threatening the port cities of Funan. Despite the Chinese role in Funan trade, the dominant cultural influence in Funan was not Chinese at all; it was Indian.

The Cham kingdom to the north of Funan had adopted many of the beliefs and customs of the Indian traders who dropped anchor in Cham harbors. The Khmer of Funan were also intrigued by the philosophical teachings and religious beliefs of the Indian traders with whom they came in contact. They began to worship the Hindu gods Shiva and Vishnu, and adopted the Indian writing system known as Sanskrit. Through Sanskrit literature, the Khmer became familiar with the myths and legends of India and Hindu sacred texts. The Khmer also incorporated their own legends and history into the Indian mythology, forming a uniquely Cambodian culture.

By the sixth century A.D., Funan was losing some of its vitality. The last known king of Funan, Rudravarman, disappears

This sandstone sculpture of a Funan deity was excavated at Oc-Eo. Funan's merchants engaged in trade along the coast of Southeast Asia.

from records about A.D. 550. Whether in response to the hostility of the Cham and Vietnamese to the north or to the changing nature of trade in the region, the center of Khmer civilization shifted inland.

ZHEN-LA

The kingdom that succeeded Funan is also known only from the name by which Chinese travelers recorded it. Zhen-La replaces Funan in Chinese records after the sixth century. The capital of the kingdom of Zhen-La, called Bhavapura, is believed to have been located in the province of Kompong Thom near the Tonle Sap. The economic life of this kingdom relied more on agriculture than on trade. The Khmer had already developed sophisticated methods of irrigation and were already relying on the waters of the Tonle Sap and man-made reservoirs to irrigate their rice crops during the dry season.

The development of irrigation techniques meant that the Khmer could harvest a much larger rice crop. A division of labor arose, and a sophisticated Zhen-La social structure evolved with Indianized priests who could read and write Sanskrit, councillors to the royal court, and local rulers to enforce the king's will. The king's greatest asset was control of the wells and the irrigation ducts that watered the fields during the dry season.

Because of Khmer inscriptions dating from this period and the location of Zhen-La, it is sometimes said that Zhen-La is the first truly Cambodian state. Cambodian society was certainly advancing quickly, and a lively interplay of Khmer culture and Indian influence marked a unique society. It is possible, however, that Zhen-La was not a unified kingdom at all, but a series of smaller kingdoms centered around waterways and reservoirs. In their records, the Chinese distinguish between a water Zhen-La and a land Zhen-La. These may have been distinct kingdoms or distinct regions of the same kingdom.

THE KHMER EMPIRE

In the year A.D. 802, a Khmer prince with the royal name of Jayavarman II ascended the hills of Phnom Kulen to the north of the Tonle Sap and proclaimed himself the *devaraja*, or god-king, of Cambodia. Signifying his triumph in defeat-

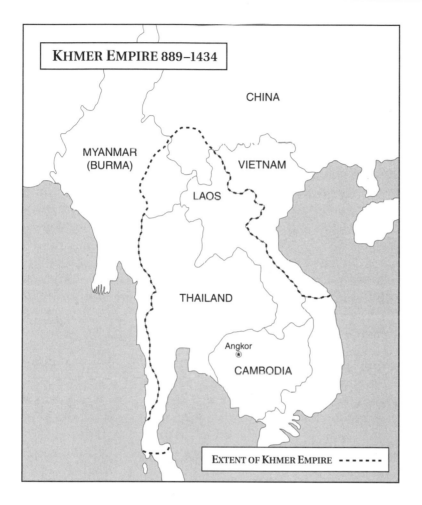

KHMER EMPIRE 889–1434

CHINA

MYANMAR
(BURMA)

VIETNAM

LAOS

THAILAND

Angkor

CAMBODIA

EXTENT OF KHMER EMPIRE - - - - - - -

ing the various local kings and military leaders of Cambodia, Jayavarman II became known as the universal monarch.

Jayavarman II was certainly an extraordinary leader. Unfortunately, only a fragmentary record of his adventures has survived. In his youth, he was either imprisoned or in exile on the Indonesian island of Java. After returning from Java, he spent his energies uniting Cambodia through diplomacy and war. He not only subdued the feuding factions that divided Cambodia, but drove from its borders foreign armies and meddlers. For his efforts, Jayavarman II is considered the first leader of a unified Cambodia.

Jayavarman II established his capital at Hariharalaya, southeast of the modern town of Siem Reap. The site is known today as Roluos and is marked by some of the oldest temples in the Angkor region. This new god-king of Cambodia fashioned himself in the likeness of Shiva, the creator and destroyer of Hindu mythology. He fashioned statues in his own likeness which tied him to Shiva and created elaborate ceremonies to make himself appear more like a god. The ascension of Jayavarman II marks the end of the Zhen-La states and the beginning of the Angkor period, during which the Khmer ruled the most powerful empire in Southeast Asia and constructed some of the world's most remarkable buildings.

Building was almost a mania with the Khmer leaders. The construction of large civic building projects and temples was pursued by king after king, both to show devotion to the gods and the former kings and to expand the scope of the imperial cities. The third king of this new empire, Indravarman I, proclaimed that he would "begin to dig five days after his coronation."[5] Indravarman created the first classical city of the Angkor age, fashioning Hariharalaya into a marvelous city of temples, administrative buildings, and waterworks. He constructed the first Angkorean reservoir, or *baray*, that would be such an important part of the agricultural life of the empire. Indravarman did not neglect to honor the previous rulers, immortalizing Jayavarman, the first god-king, in a statuary likeness of the god Shiva.

Indravarman's son, Yashovarman I, continued the building mania of his father and began construction of a new imperial city. It was named Yashodharapura in honor of its founder, but is known to history as Angkor. The word *Angkor* is derived from the Khmer version of the Sanskrit word *nagara*, which means "holy city." It was located north of Siem Reap, just beyond the highest point of the floodwaters of the Tonle Sap. Indravarman had constructed the first of the two enormous barays at Angkor. This reservoir measured four miles (over seven kilometers) east to west and one mile (just less than two kilometers) north to south. Equally impressive, the west baray was later added. Between the barays lay the central part of the city of Angkor.

The focal point of the great city was a temple-mountain, a feature that characterized Angkor religious sites. The temple mount uses an existing hill for its foundation. The temple rises from this foundation in a succession of progressively smaller steps that lends the structure the appearance of a step-pyramid. The temple is crowned by a building with a

A statue of the Hindu god Shiva performing the dance of creation. Khmer kings considered themselves earthly incarnations of this omnipotent deity.

door, known as a tower sanctuary. The temple-mountain at the heart of Angkor is symbolic of Mount Meru, the mythical axis of the world in Buddhist theology. In other words, Angkor was meant to be a representation of the very center of the universe.

It might seem surprising that the Angkorean builders, busily constructing temples to Hindu gods and decorating them with bas-relief versions of Hindu scriptural texts, should suddenly celebrate the teachings of the Buddha. In fact, it is one of the curiosities of Angkorean society that Hindu and Buddhist beliefs coexisted. Both religions originated in India and were adopted by the Khmer. Some rulers strongly preferred one but

TIMELESS INSCRIPTIONS

The inscriptions and bas-relief carvings on the stone temples of Cambodia are the primary source of the history of Cambodia in the Angkorean age. The damp, tropical climate of Cambodia saturated and destroyed records written on paper and wood. The inscriptions in Sanskrit and the slightly raised carvings of the walls of temples gave archaeologists a key to Cambodia's ancient links with India.

Aside from telling of the Khmer kings and their triumphs in battle, the temple carvings recount the legends, sagas, myths, and epics of Hindu India. Representations of Shiva the destroyer, elephant-headed Ganesha, and Brahma with his four mouths, are all carved on temples in Cambodia. These Hindu gods were kept company by a vast number of lesser gods and demons. Carved in Sanskrit, the language of Hindu priests, the great epics of India—the *Mahabharata* and the *Ramayana*—also adorn the buildings of Angkor. Verses from the epic poems tied the Khmer people to the greatness of India and created a mythology that mixed Khmer and Indian cultures to form something uniquely Cambodian.

not usually to the complete exclusion of the other. Statues of the kings of Angkor, therefore, were carved in the likeness of the Buddha and the gods of the Hindu pantheon.

The Angkorean empire was never static. It was marked by repeated periods of war and conquest. The armies of Angkor clashed with the Thai to the west, the Vietnamese to the east, and the Lao peoples in what is today Laos to the north. At the height of the Angkor empire, all three peoples fell subject to the rule of the Khmer, who looted their riches and captured them as slaves. Angkor became a rich city with a vast imperial bureaucracy of priests and councillors to the king. A Chinese envoy, Zhou Daguan, who spent 1296 and 1297 in Angkor, recorded the splendor of a royal procession:

> When the King leaves his palace, the procession is headed by the soldiery; then come the flags, the banners, the music. Girls of the palace, three or five hun-

dred in number, gaily dressed, with flowers in their hair and tapers in their hands, are massed together in a separate column. . . . Finally the Sovereign appeared, standing erect on an elephant and holding in his hand the sacred sword. This elephant, his tusks sheathed in gold, was accompanied by bearers of twenty white parasols with golden shafts. All around was a bodyguard of elephants, drawn close together.[6]

THE CRUMBLING OF AN EMPIRE

The Khmer were indeed masters of ceremony. The splendor of their civilization seemed to keep pace with its rapid expansion. During the reign of Suryavarman II (1113–1150), Khmer armies subjugated the great maritime state of Champa in southern Vietnam. At Angkor, Suryavarman II began the construction of a great temple, Angkor Wat. He dedicated the temple to the Hindu god Vishnu. It is perhaps his greatest contribution to Angkor civilization, for it is considered to represent the high point of Angkorean architecture;

An enormous statue of a seated Buddha rests intact among the ruins of Lop Buri in Thailand. Lop Buri was a capital city in the Khmer empire.

ANGKOR WAT

Considered to be the finest of all Angkorean buildings, Angkor Wat was built in the early twelfth century during the reign of Suryavarman II. It is thought to be dedicated to the Hindu god Vishnu, but may have been intended as a mausoleum for the god-king Suryavarman.

Angkor Wat served as the main temple of the capital city, Angkor. Its scale is enormous, covering 500 acres (210 hectares). To reach the main temple, one must cross a causeway that spans a lake-like moat. The moat is 650 feet (200 meters) wide and acts as a reflecting pool for the temple. The five great towers that rise from Angkor Wat's top level mirror the lotus buds sprouting from the moat below. The entire complex is made from sandstone quarried in the region. Running along the outer edges of the complex are covered galleries that provide relief from the heat of the sun's rays. The outer walls are also covered with bas-reliefs carved into the sandstone and depicting epic battles in Hindu mythology and exploits of Suryavarman II.

all the skills that the Khmer builders had been honing over the years were brought to a perfect pitch in the creation of this one great temple. It is splendid in scale, but remarkably subtle in its details.

Suryavarman II's reign had been brilliantly successful, but the Cham nursed their hatred of the invading Khmer and longed to avenge the humiliation of defeat. Their chance came in 1177. Suryavarman II had already died, but the Cham were happy to take their revenge on his successors. The Cham, a seafaring kingdom, resorted to water assault. They dispatched their navy up the Mekong until it branched off at Phnom Penh into the Sap River. Their little armada caught the Khmer off guard. They not only looted Angkor, causing much death and destruction, but also took the head of the king.

In 1181, the last of the great kings of Angkor ascended the throne. King Jayavarman VII succeeded in defeating the Cham in a naval battle and fortifying the city of Angkor. He strengthened the walls and made many other practical improvements for security. He also built the temple of Bayon, the last of the large Angkorean temple complexes. The bas-reliefs on the Bayon temple reflected the king's devotion to Buddhism and his concern for his subjects, for whom he built hospitals for the body and temples for the soul. After the death of Jayavarman VII around A.D. 1220, no more significant buildings were added to Angkor.

The empire entered a period of decline. Many theories have been put forth for the decline of Angkor. Some scholars point out that the great reservoirs at Angkor became blocked with silt, leading to a decline in the central control of water. The construction of new types of bridges that could be closed off to form dams supports this theory, since the new dams were not necessarily built near Angkor and therefore dispersed power.

Another factor in the decline of Angkor was the rising might of Vietnam and Thailand. After more than four hundred years

This giant smiling face is one of nearly two hundred such sculptures in the Bayon temple complex. Bayon was the last Angkorean temple built.

as the most powerful kingdom in Southeast Asia, Cambodia found itself eclipsed by the growing power of its neighbors. Much resentment toward the mighty Khmer had built up over the years. The Khmer suffered military defeats at the hands of the Vietnamese and the Thai and saw their empire shrink. In 1431, Thai armies struck into the heart of the Khmer empire, sacking Angkor itself.

The Khmer royals responded to the kingdom's new hardships by migrating downstream on the Sap River to found a new capital north of Phnom Penh. By the end of the fifteenth century, Angkor's role as the administrative and spiritual heart of the Khmer empire ended entirely. The greatness of the Angkorean age faded, and the jungle began to slowly retake the once flourishing city. When Henri Mahout visited the ruins of Angkor in 1860, the buildings of the city appeared to sprout from within the jungle, so completely had Angkor been swallowed up by the jungle. The main inhabitants when Mahout entered Angkor were monks who had established a Buddhist monastery on the grounds of the abandoned temples.

With the passing of the great age of Angkor, Cambodia entered a long period of decline and struggle. No longer would it play a role as the great power of Southeast Asia; instead, it would struggle for survival against competing foreign powers.

THE ROAD TO
INDEPENDENCE

4

The modern nation of Cambodia is essentially the product of a long struggle to determine what form Cambodia would take after the fall of the Angkor civilization. This struggle was often violent, with the arrival of outside armies and ideas that caused great upheaval in Cambodia.

Between the time that Angkor was abandoned in the fifteenth century and the arrival of the French in the nineteenth century, the Khmer empire withered like the Tonle Sap in the dry season. The borders of the empire slowly constricted as the influence of the Khmer lessened. No one is sure exactly why, but slowly and surely Khmer influence waned and the nation of Cambodia became a shadow of its former self.

The capital was moved from Angkor southeast along the Sap River to Lovek, north of Phnom Penh. The location was a strategic choice in that it was distant from both the Vietnamese and Thai borders. The capital at Lovek had none of the splendor of Angkor. No great temples were built and no massive *barays*. The days of the great builders were over. Even the quarries where sandstone was hewn from the earth in giant blocks for the building projects of Angkor were nearly abandoned.

THE OPENING OF MARITIME TRADE

Lovek, however, proved to be a thriving trading city. The decline of Angkor coincided with the rise of trade with China. Some scholars have argued that the growing importance of a maritime trading economy hastened the fall of Angkor, pulling the energies of the Khmer in new directions and shifting their focus toward the south of the country, where the waters of the Mekong carried trade goods to the sea.

At the center of Lovek's commercial community were Chinese immigrants who had settled in Cambodia to facilitate their business enterprises and who generally lived in cities along the Mekong, the commercial highway of the region. Chinese involvement in trading enterprises and small businesses in Cambodia became a marked feature of Cambodian society and continues to this day. Only during the upheaval of the Khmer Rouge rule in the 1970s was the pattern interrupted, only to begin again after the fall of Pol Pot's government.

The Chinese imported goods such as silk, which the nobles used to make their garments, and weapons. Primary exports included spices and gold, which were measured out in Chinese units of measurement, for Cambodians adopted the weights and measures of imperial China. The Chinese, however, were not the only ones to prosper from the increase of maritime trade. Indian, Malay, and Indonesian captains all piloted ships to the coastal region of Lower

SILK ROAD ON THE SEA

The Silk Road is probably the most famous caravan route in history. It stretched from China in the east to Rome in the west and resulted in the exchange of goods and ideas between two of the world's greatest empires and the many peoples and cultures that connected them.

Recent excavations along Egypt's Red Sea coast have revealed the presence of great maritime trading cities that acted as transit points for goods moving across the desert to be taken down the Nile to the Mediterranean or loaded on ships heading east. This maritime route is thought to rival the Silk Road, shipping goods between China and Rome. After stops along the Arabian coast and India, ships are thought to have reached the Chinese port city of Canton in the Pearl River estuary in southern China. The ships would probably have dropped anchor along the coast of Vietnam and possibly Cambodia. The Khmer Krom region in what is now Cambodia may well have been a part of this trade route. The Cambodians traded with both India and China through established trade lanes of the seas. It may be that Cambodia was a link on the Silk Road on the sea.

Cambodia (South Vietnam) or sailed up the Mekong to sell their wares. The greatness of the Cambodian empire might have passed, but the royal families of Cambodia still lived lavishly, partly from maritime profits. Khmer royalty and other Cambodian nobles involved themselves in the international trade enterprises just as investors would today. They still collected taxes from the rice crops and fees from water usage, but this new economy presented a way to make up for lost taxes on a shrinking kingdom.

During this period of decline for the Khmer empire, two new religious movements played a role in shaping life in Cambodia. Islam came from India, where it had become a strong rival in the north to Hinduism. Its spread was hastened by Muslim sailors from India. The religion attracted many converts, especially among populations who had not previously converted to Buddhism or Hinduism from their traditional pagan or animistic beliefs. Islam offered the converts a formal, highly organized religion with clear moral principles and structured rituals of worship and conduct. Like Christians, Muslims worshiped only one god, Allah, whose prophet, Muhammad, is said to have written down Allah's teachings in the Koran. The Koran is the holy book of Islam, and because it was first written in Arabic, Muslims also believe that Arabic is a holy language.

Through the sea routes, Muslim sailors spread their religion to Indonesia, Malaysia, and the Cham community of Lower Cambodia. Because of their importance to the commerce of the region, Muslim Cham became important councillors at the courts of Cambodian royals. They provided the Chinese with fierce competition and sometimes powerful allies in the struggle to control the profitable maritime trade of the Mekong.

THERAVADA BUDDHISM

While Islam spread by sea, a new form of Buddhism was taking hold among the Khmer. Historian David Chandler argues that the spread of Theravada Buddhism was the most important change in Cambodia between the thirteenth and fifteenth centuries, a time when the Khmer empire was fading. As a religious movement it was a stunning success. Today, more than 90 percent of all Cambodians are adherents of the Theravada sect of Buddhism.

A Theravada Buddhist monk worships in the Bayon temple. Theravada Buddhism spread to Cambodia from Thailand during the decline of the Khmer empire.

The teachings of Buddhism originated with the Indian prince Gautama, whom followers had taken to calling the "enlightened one," or Buddha. Eight centuries after Gautama's death around 480 B.C., Buddhists on the teardrop-shaped island of Sri Lanka initiated a reform movement that became known as Theravada. It was an attempt to rid Buddhism of the ornate trappings it had picked up over the years, partly due to the influence of Hinduism, with its plentiful pantheon of gods and demigods. While Hinduism allowed for ornate rituals and many greater and lesser dieties, the Theravada Buddhists focused almost exclusively on scripture, the sacred religious texts of Buddhism. Theravada monks taught that individual righteousness could provide an escape from the torment of the world's sufferings, which were repeated again and again in the Buddhist cycle of rebirth. According to Buddhism, the soul is reborn over and over again in different forms, in painful but necessary steps toward enlightenment. Theravada monks taught that those who wished to escape the painful cycle must lead simple lives of devotion, meditation, and detachment.

Theravada Buddhism spread from Sri Lanka to India, Burma (Myanmar), and Thailand. From Thailand, monks draped in the same reddish robes that they wear today wandered into Cambodia carrying their message of hope. Their beliefs spread quickly among ordinary Cambodians. Part of the appeal of their teachings was that ordinary people could have the same access to salvation as the rich and powerful. Through simple acts of selflessness, the path to enlightenment was assured. Hinduism, though surviving in the national mythology of Cambodia, died out as a living religion.

SHIPS FROM THE WEST

In the sixteenth century, a new religion arrived in Cambodia. The new religion was Christianity. Missionaries had arrived

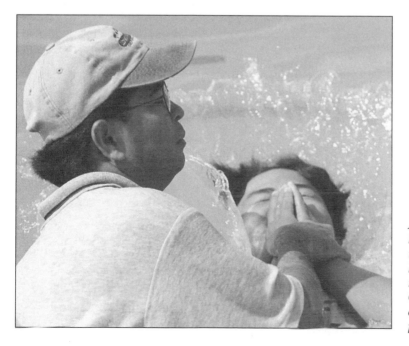

A Cambodian pastor baptizes a young woman. Christianity has historically been a minority religion in Cambodia, and today only one percent of the population is Christian.

in the Far East along with the trading expeditions that marked the European Age of Exploration. The Portuguese, for example, set up a rich trading city at the mouth of the Pearl River in Southern China. Their rivals and fellow Catholics, the Spanish, competed with Portuguese missionaries in the region, and they were soon followed by other Europeans. The Christian missionaries puzzled the kings of Cambodia, who tolerated their attempts to convert the followers of Buddha. For the most part, however, the missionaries failed in Cambodia. Buddhism was not only the major religion of Cambodia, but had become part of the Cambodian identity. Christian missionaries simply could not convince Cambodians to abandon it for a new religion. Only small groups, generally of non-Khmer minorities, converted to Christianity.

The European entry into the power politics of Southeast Asia, however, proved to have a longer-lasting effect. The Cambodian royal court at Lovek cautiously welcomed the Europeans, hoping to profit from trade with the newcomers and to use their military prowess against enemies of Cambodia. Thus, the Spanish and Portuguese missionaries and merchants joined the cosmopolitan communities of Lovek and Phnom Penh. Their languages added to the babel of the already polyglot communities of Chinese, Vietnamese, Japanese, Malays, Indonesians, Indians, and Arabs.

The Khmer rulers hoped the newcomers would be useful allies in their struggle against the Thai and Vietnamese. Cambodia had been in constant conflict with Thailand since the fall of Angkor. But the Thai had grown increasingly powerful, and the Cambodian king feared that Thailand would launch a ruinous invasion of the rump kingdom of Cambodia. King Satha of Cambodia appealed to the Spanish to send troops in return for trade privileges and a free rein for missionaries. By the time two Spanish adventurers arrived in Lovek, however, Satha had been overthrown by a Cambodian rival. Spanish troops were to follow, but not before the Thai sacked Lovek in 1597.

STRUGGLE FOR EXISTENCE

For the next couple of centuries, Cambodia struggled for its very existence. The Spanish, whose garrison at Lovek was massacred in 1599, proved not to be the answer Cambodians were looking for. Instead, Cambodia lived at the mercy of the hostile rulers of Thailand and Vietnam. Cambodia was caught in a vise between these two powers, squeezed nearly to death. The pressure on Cambodia was relieved only by the preoccupations of the enemy kingdoms. Thai ambitions to their east were checked by Burmese attacks from the west. Burma had also come into its own as a military force, and harried the Thai armies whenever they had the chance. Khmer forces, for example, had once reached the capital of the powerful kingdom of Ayuthaya only to find the Burmese installed as conquerors. The Burmese were unable to hold on to Thailand, just as the Thai were unable to hold on to Cambodia. Thailand did, however, gain control of much of western Cambodia, including Battambang and Angkor, for much of the seventeenth and eighteenth centuries.

In the eastern part of the country, Cambodia clashed with the increasingly hostile Vietnamese. The Vietnamese had long despised their neighbors in Cambodia, believing them to be uncivilized and inferior. Vietnamese attitudes were partly the result of the very different forces that shaped the two nations. Vietnam had adopted the imperial and bureaucratic traditions of the Chinese. They emulated the greatness of the Chinese empire. They also inherited the xenophobic views of the Chinese. They believed themselves and their culture to be superior to others in Southeast Asia.

This chauvinistic attitude manifested itself in territorial ambitions in Lower Cambodia, which today forms the southernmost part of Vietnam. The Khmer of this region were under siege from the neighboring Vietnamese. The Vietnamese were slowly settling in the region, and their numbers soon outstripped the ethnic Khmer. In the 1620s the Vietnamese settled in the village of Prey Nokor, which subsequently grew into South Vietnam's most important city, Saigon. The Vietnamese made no secret of their ambition to annex the Khmer Krom. The rulers of southern Vietnam were the Nguyen Lords, one of the two great dynasties that ruled Vietnam. The Nguyen Lords offered assistance to the Cambodian government in fending off the Thai advances. In return, they claimed the Khmer Krom for Vietnam.

GUNBOAT DIPLOMACY

In the nineteenth century, Cambodia became a pawn in the great race of colonizers arriving in Asia by sea. The rapid scientific developments of the Industrial Revolution had enabled the Western powers to harness the explosive properties of gunpowder into ferocious military firepower. On their ships they mounted cannons, which protected them from pirates on the sea and allowed them to bombard foreign ports in a show of might. The use of force and threats of force by the Western colonial powers became known as gunboat diplomacy.

In the late nineteenth century, the Western powers seemed to be closing in on Cambodia. The British added Burma, present-day Myanmar, to their colonial holdings in India; the Dutch established colonies in Indonesia and Malaysia; and the Americans, former colonials themselves, ousted the Spanish from the Philippines. When the French first arrived in Cambodia to negotiate a settlement, one of the reasons that they took Cambodia for France was simply because no one else had claimed it for themselves.

It was clear to all that the Cambodians were trapped between the Thai to the west and the Vietnamese to the east. However, they lacked the power to do little more than turn the Vietnamese and Thai against each other. Moreover, just as the Thai were often preoccupied by war with the Burmese, the Vietnamese had their own troubles. The Nguyen Lords had a rival in Vietnam—the Trinh Lords, who occupied the territory in northern Vietnam. The clash of these two rivals took pressure off the Cambodians. It also drove the Nguyen Lords farther south into the Mekong Delta, traditionally territory of the Khmer.

By the nineteenth century, Cambodia's situation was desperate. Usurpers, pretenders to the throne, and ambitious generals all schemed for the throne and courted the friendship of foreign powers to back them as ruler of Cambodia. No king could survive for long without the help of a foreign power. By the 1830s, the Vietnamese had gained the upper hand in Cambodia. The Vietnamese emperor, Minh Mang, recommended that his representatives in Cambodia should civilize the Cambodians by teaching them manners. "The barbarians in Cambodia," Minh Mang wrote, "have become my children."[7] Minh Mang's arrogance might have been tempered had he known that Vietnam too would be ruled by a foreign power in a very short time.

FRENCH INDOCHINA

Cambodia might have ceased to be a state had not it been for the entry of a new power into the Southeast Asian political arena. The French seized on political instability in Cambodia to establish their own influence in the country. The French interest in Cambodia was an outgrowth of existing French influence in Vietnam. French missionaries had had much more success in Vietnam than the Spanish did in Cambodia. And in 1809, the Vietnamese emperor Gia Long awarded the French certain privileges in Vietnam, partly for their help in putting down a rebellion. Vietnamese conversion to Christianity, however, alarmed his successors.

The Vietnamese emperors in the imperial capital of Hue tried to snuff out the growing Christian influence. The French responded by dispatching gunboats to seize Vietnam by force of arms. On February 17, 1859, the French forces captured Saigon, which they made a base of operations for further expansion. By 1884 the French had planted colonial representatives in all the major towns of Vietnam and secured for the emperor of France a new colony.

A statue of Minh Mang at the emperor's tomb in Hue, Vietnam. The Vietnamese ruled Cambodia during the first half of the nineteenth century.

Had the French been content to limit their colonial holdings to Vietnam, the implications for Cambodia would still have been enormous. No longer could the mighty Nguyen Lords launch expeditions into Cambodia. The Vietnamese military was subordinated to French colonial officers. Because the Cambodian ruler, King Norodom, had been installed by agreement between the Thai and Vietnamese governments, the French naturally involved themselves in the foreign policy of Vietnam, their new colony.

In August 1863 the French dispatched well-armed representatives to compel King Norodom to sign a treaty with the
French, relinquishing the king's right to decide questions of
foreign policy. As a figurehead ruler, Norodom did not exercise much power and readily signed the document presented by the French. It gave the French control over
Cambodian foreign policy and installed in the Cambodian
capital a *resident superior,* or French consul, to oversee
French interests. To accommodate the Thai, the French allowed the provinces of Battambang and Siem Reap to be
governed by representatives of the Thai court.

MISSION CIVILISATRICE

Thirty years after taking control in Cambodia, the French
took control of the Lao tribes to the north of Cambodia. They
reasoned that Laos would make a good buffer for Vietnam,
which was their primary interest in Southeast Asia. The three
states of Vietnam, Laos, and Cambodia made up French Indochina. To justify their presence in Indochina, the French
claimed a *mission civilisatrice*, a civilizing mission. They
claimed, mostly for the benefit of interested citizens back in
France, that they intended to bring Christianity and good
government to the barbaric peoples of Southeast Asia.

There is of course much cynicism in the French claim that
they were in Indochina for the good of the local peoples. It is
true that French missionaries believed in their mission—to
bring the light of Christianity to the dark realm of the heathen,
as they saw it. But in Cambodia the missionaries failed miser-
ably, and most colonial administrators had no illusions that
they were in Indochina for any reason other than to exploit the
land for the benefit of France. Moreover, they believed that
Cambodia provided a useful buffer state, insulating Vietnam,
the jewel of French Indochina, from Burma (Myanmar),
which the English had drawn into the fold of their own empire.
Even if the British succeeded in colonizing Thailand—which
they never did—French Vietnam would still be separated from
the British sphere of influence by Cambodia.

The one group of Frenchmen who did have a positive effect on Cambodia were the scientists—archaeologists, histo-
rians, geologists, engineers—who studied and catalogued the
great Angkorean civilization. Many of the French who ex-

THE WONDER HOUSE OF PHNOM PENH

Although the French were responsible for shipping many beautiful works of Khmer art out of Cambodia to museums and private collections abroad, they preserved some of the finest pieces for a collection in Phnom Penh. To house the collection they designed an elegant building with the steep roofs and stupa-like crowns of Cambodian architecture. The building was painted a reddish color resembling the color of monks' robes. This building, opened in 1918, became the National Museum. Remarkably, the museum and its collection survived the Khmer Rouge—who destroyed many fine works of art—and the subsequent years of civil war. It is today a national treasure of Cambodia and one of the positive legacies of French colonial rule.

plored the jungles of Cambodia searching for temples and lost cities were great admirers of the Cambodians and dealt sympathetically with local people. They learned Khmer and Sanskrit, studied local customs and folklore, and wrote down their findings. Slowly they pieced together a picture of Cambodia's forgotten past. Since most records written on anything but stone had disintegrated in the water-laden climate of Cambodia, the French scholars relied primarily on the inscriptions and bas-reliefs decorating the many stone buildings of Angkorean ruins. Through their research, the French pieced together the history of Angkor, which had been forgotten even by Cambodians. When the greatness and splendor of Angkor emerged in French scholarship, the Cambodians were perhaps more startled than anyone.

Unintentionally, French scholarship helped foster Cambodian nationalism. The greatness of the Cambodian past, retold to Cambodians by the French, kindled feelings of pride in being Cambodian. The importance of the Angkorean past grew, and is evident in the present-day political use of the great temple of Angkor Wat. For example, *Angkor Wat* was the name of Cambodia's most important early nationalist newspaper, and a stylized representation of the silhouette of Angkor Wat has been used on the flags of every government that has ruled Cambodia in the twentieth century.

The French shaped Cambodians' perceptions of their country in another important way. The French were ardent supporters of Cambodia's royal family and did much to increase the visibility of the Cambodian royals. The French preferred to exercise their control over Cambodia from behind the scenes. To carry out their policies, however, they needed a strong central leader. That leader was the king. To demonstrate to Cambodians that the king was an important and powerful head of state, the French treated the Cambodian monarch with great respect and allowed him to live a lavish lifestyle, hoping that the pomp and spectacle would impress the average Cambodian.

Tourists photograph the Royal Palace in Phnom Penh. The French established Phnom Penh as the capital of Cambodia in 1865.

The French rule of Cambodia was largely peaceful and comparatively uneventful. One significant change was the relocation of the capital from Udong, where it had moved from Lovek, to the city of Phnom Penh at the intersection of the Sap, Mekong, and Basac Rivers. The city was primarily a center for Chinese trade along the Mekong. The French, who called the area *Quatre Bras*, or "Four Arms," preferred Phnom Penh because it could be reached directly by river from Saigon, the center of French administration in southern Vietnam. The city subsequently flourished. Architects constructed a palace for the royals, elegant avenues with European-style buildings, and many temples to celebrate the new status of the city.

Under the French, the kings of Cambodia were all descended from the same family. The first was King Norodom, who had signed the treaty that attached Cambodia to French Indochina. Norodom's great-grandson Norodom Sihanouk is the most notable of the modern Cambodian kings. After being chosen by the French to be king, he led the nationalist sentiment that helped sweep the French from Cambodia. He then resigned his royal title and entered the ring as a politician. Sinanouk proved to be a wily politician, adept at survival and political reincarnation. In many respects, he is the father of the modern Cambodian state.

5

STRUGGLE
FOR SURVIVAL

King Norodom Sihanouk would preside over the birth of the modern Cambodian state, proclaiming independence for his long-suffering people. Cambodia in the twentieth century, however, experienced horrors that afflict few other nations. In the midst of political upheavals, international conflicts, and civil war, Cambodia struggled to emerge as a modern nation. That passage has been one of the most painful and violent births of any country on earth. When foreign armies were not bombing, or marching over, Cambodian territory, the Cambodians let loose on themselves, first through civil war and then through the genocidal regime of the Khmer Rouge, a regime that killed one in seven people in Cambodia.

THE CRUMBLING OF INDOCHINA

The two men who have had the greatest influence on Cambodia in the twentieth century are Pol Pot and King Norodom Sihanouk. Both achieved great power but their methods were utterly different. Pol Pot embraced a single fanatical ideology and ruthlessly practiced it. Sihanouk, in contrast, was a political acrobat, swinging from one position to the next as support and alliances shifted. He has played a role in nearly every major movement in modern Cambodian history, variously puppet king, independence leader, populist politician, right-wing strongman, leftist reformer, political exile, nationalist liberator, and royal figurehead. Most of all, through the uncertainty of modern Cambodian history, Sihanouk provided a link to the past. For some, he became a living symbol of Cambodian nationhood.

The upheaval brought about by the outbreak of World War II gave Sihanouk his chance to be king. The French chose Sihanouk to be the king of Cambodia in 1941, passing over his father in the belief that the nineteen-year-old prince would be more pliable. France itself had been occupied by Nazi Germany in 1940 and the French government that administered Cambodia was the collaborationist French government set up at the town of Vichy. The Vichy regime was nominally allied with the Japanese, who had conquered much of Southeast Asia in their own military drive.

The Japanese allowed the French colonial administrators to remain at their posts because of the arrangement that the Axis powers—Germany, Austria, Fascist Italy and Japan—had come to with Vichy France. In reality, the Japanese simply tolerated the French administrators because they were short of men to replace them. When the Allied powers invaded France in 1944, toppling the Vichy government, the Japanese arrested the French officials in Cambodia. By the following year, the Japanese empire itself was crumbling. Sihanouk accepted a Japanese offer of independence for Cambodia with himself as king. For five months, Sihanouk ruled Cambodia as head of

King Sihanouk (left) converses with the French colonial secretary. Sihanouk came to power as a puppet of the French who through him continued to control Cambodia.

state. It was a first taste of independence, albeit in a world at war and though Cambodia was still occupied by foreign soldiers.

In the aftermath of World War II, calls for independence came from European colonies around the globe. The Allied war aim of making the world safe for democracy and defeating the tyranny of Nazism and fascism left the colonial powers in an awkward position at the war's end. How could nations who were claiming to have won the war in the name of democracy deny their colonial subjects democratic freedoms? Nevertheless, the French returned to Indochina, hoping to recolonize and carry on as if nothing had changed. But things had changed. Opposition to the French colonial rule began to form. In Vietnam, the French faced outright rebellion from the Vietnamese. In Cambodia, opposition simmered. The main opponents of French rule were Cambodians seeking to establish a democracy and a small group of Cambodian Communists, who were aligned with Communists from other parts of Indochina, notably Vietnam.

King Sihanouk welcomed the French back into Cambodia, not ready to oppose them. He lived a good life with French backing. Like his ancestors, King Sihanouk relied on the French to support him. He provided a national symbol for Cambodia while the French provided the army to keep him in power. During these years Sihanouk visited France, and there was much that he liked about it. "I am an anticolonialist," he said, "but if one must be colonized, it is better to be colonized by gourmets."[8]

Nevertheless, when Sihanouk realized that the majority of Cambodians were opposed to French rule, he championed the anticolonial cause. It was the first of his many reincarnations. Like the Hindu gods of Angkor, Sihanouk emerged as a leader with a new face, claiming always to be a protector of the people. The French, bogged down in increasingly bloody colonial war in Vietnam, decided that Cambodia was not worth fighting for. Perhaps as a final act of *mission civilisatrice,* the French encouraged the growth of political parties in Cambodia and allowed Cambodia to form a National Assembly, composed of elected delegates from different political parties. The main party, the Democratic Party, wanted a parliamentary government. Many also wanted to topple the monarchy and establish a republic. Fearing that Cambodians were about to oust the royal family, Sihanouk launched his own campaign—the Royal Campaign for Independence—to win over the people's support. The king succeeded in winning popular support, but many politicians still called for a republic. Sihanouk turned to the French to stamp out the republican sentiment. In 1952, with French backing, the king dissolved the nascent National Assembly, ending Cambodia's brief experiment with democracy.

THE KINGDOM OF CAMBODIA

In 1953 the French agreed to renounce all involvement in Cambodia. Sihanouk proclaimed the creation of the independent kingdom of Cambodia, which he ruled with nearly unlimited power. While Sihanouk reinforced his own authority, however, he professed a belief that the future of Cambodia lay with the will of the electorate. For the first time in their history Cambodians would be permitted to decide what kind of government they wanted.

King Sihanouk touches the hands of schoolchildren during a 2001 independence day celebration.

According to international agreements signed in 1954 in Geneva, Switzerland, which formally recognized the independence of Cambodia, elections would be held in 1955 to reestablish the National Assembly. Sihanouk was determined to retain control of Cambodian politics and not just as a figurehead. Sihanouk was already the most famous Cambodian, and to capitalize on his popularity he formed his own left-leaning political party, the Sangkum Reastr Nyum (People's Socialist Community). Sihanouk wanted to use this political party to gather support among average Cambodians, promising in particular to help Cambodia's farmers and common laborers. Realizing, however, that he could not run for office as king of the country, Sihanouk abdicated. He placed on his throne his father, Suramarit, to serve as figurehead, and entered the political arena as an ex-king.

It was a stroke of political genius. Prince Sihanouk, as he was known after his abdication, could now enter the fray of politics. Moreover, despite his abdication, he carried the aura of nobility into his campaign against commoners for a government post. In fact, as a former king and leader of Cambodian independence, Sihanouk was seen as divine by many Cambodians. The Sangkum won every seat in the National Assembly, and Sihanouk became prime minister of Cambodia at the head of a political party that had no opposition in the government.

The Sangkum controlled the assembly for the next fifteen years, and Sihanouk ruled Cambodia from a position of nearly absolute control. He involved himself in every aspect of the Cambodian state. He directed movies starring himself. He held elaborate opera performances at the ruins of Angkor to impress foreign dignitaries. More seriously, he encouraged economic growth. Under Sihanouk's rule, the government played a direct role in managing the economy and running state-owned businesses. Some were successes, others failures. The high-profile Sihanouk was an inveterate booster, for himself in Cambodia and for Cambodia abroad. His support for the poor in Cambodia seems to have been genuine, and many rural villages supported him. Nevertheless, opposition to Sihanouk's rule grew.

WAR AND REBELLION

One of Sihanouk's weaknesses was surrounding himself with yes-men, appointees who agreed with his every word but offered little reasoned advice or practical experience in running the country. Had he had advisers who depicted Cambodia's political situation honestly, Sihanouk would have seen a bleak picture. Two groups of opponents were gaining strength and both wanted to rid Cambodia of Sihanouk and the royal family. On the political spectrum, the groups represented the far left and the far right. Sihanouk would be squeezed in the middle. On the left, the opposition wanted to rid Cambodia of a royal family, whom they saw as oppressing the common workers. On the right, the opposition wanted to kick out the royal family and seize power for themselves. The right drew much support from the military.

On the far left were the ranks of the growing Indochina Communist Party (ICP). This left-wing organization had its roots in Vietnam, where Ho Chi Minh had led a successful guerrilla war against the French and was fighting against the U.S.-backed Republic of South Vietnam. The young Communists of the ICP had largely picked up their ideology while studying abroad. Ho Chi Minh embraced revolutionary politics in France, and his Communist ideology inspired him to fight the French back at home. Cambodian radicals took inspiration from the Vietnamese and worked closely with them to form the underground Communist Party in Cambodia. The movement at first centered around the remote and sparsely populated areas of Cambodia that bordered Vietnam. In the jungles the Communists established guerrilla training camps well supplied on trails across the Vietnamese border.

On the far right, conservative Cambodian generals and business leaders began to grumble about the prime minister. These two groups were both staunchly anti-Communist, and they both wanted more control of military and economic activities. The army wanted to expand its powers and launch campaigns to destroy the Communists operating in Cambodia's jungles and remote areas. The industrialists, including many prosperous Chinese Cambodians, wanted private ownership of businesses, arguing that the government stamped out fair competition and hurt the Cambodian economy.

Sihanouk attempted to maneuver between both sides. However, this proved difficult even for Cambodia's greatest showman. When war in Vietnam spilled over the border into Cambodia, Sihanouk lost all control. The escalation of war in Vietnam impacted Cambodia in two ways. First was the

DEATH FROM THE SKY

During the Vietnam War of the 1960s and 1970s, the American attempts to preserve the anti-Communist government of the Republic of South Vietnam against assaults from Communist North Vietnam and rebellion from local Communist insurgents had grave consequences for Cambodia. To supply Communist fighters in South Vietnam, a supply trail had been cobbled together from local roads and jungle trails. From its origin in China, the trail snaked through Laos and Cambodia, dipping into Vietnam at many points. The trail was named for the leader of North Vietnam, Ho Chi Minh, and provided a lifeline for Communist resistance fighters in South Vietnam.

To seal off the Ho Chi Minh Trail and destroy the North Vietnamese and Viet Cong bases in Cambodia, the American government authorized a secret bombing campaign against Cambodia. During the campaign, more bombs were dropped on the eastern provinces of Cambodia than in all of World War II. The widespread carpet bombing of the American B-52s killed many Cambodians and increased support for Cambodia's budding Communist Party.

presence of North Vietnamese troops on Cambodian soil. Vietnamese Communists used Cambodia as a refuge from American bombing runs. They established base camps in Cambodian territory aided by Cambodian Communists. These base camps became supply depots along a supply route that stretched from China to South Vietnam. The Ho Chi Minh Trail, as the supply route was known, attracted the attention of American military planners, who unleashed ferocious carpet-bombing raids on eastern Cambodia. The U.S. military planners hoped that this saturation bombing would destroy the North Vietnamese supply chain and force a Communist withdrawal. However, the American bombs killed indiscriminately, and numerous Cambodian civilians were among the dead.

THE LON NOL REGIME

The American carpet bombings that killed Cambodians in eastern Cambodia stirred resentment throughout Cambodian society. The reaction was swift: Cambodians turned on the Vietnamese and murdered them. Cambodian armed forces clashed with the Vietnamese and the Cambodian Communists in the eastern part of the country.

Prince Sihanouk, however, decided he had more to fear from the Americans than the North Vietnamese, and began to lend help to the North Vietnamese. He had earlier learned of a plot backed by the American Central Intelligence Agency (CIA) to overthrow him. If he would have to choose sides, he would side with the Communist Vietnamese, because he distrusted the United States. At the same time, however, he attempted to crush the Cambodian Communist Party at home. To repress the Communists, Sihanouk relied on the ultraloyal forces of General Lon Nol, the commander of the army. Lon Nol had been a longtime supporter of Sihanouk, but the army was loyal to its general, not to the prince. This became painfully clear to Sihanouk in 1970. Sihanouk was in France for medical treatment when he heard

American warplanes bomb a Vietnamese target. The U.S. military carried out similar strikes on Cambodia for providing supplies to the Communist Vietnamese.

that he had been deposed by a coup. Lon Nol had seized power with Sihanouk's cousin Prince Sisowath Matak.

Lon Nol and Prince Sisowath felt that Sihanouk had been drifting too far toward the Communist North Vietnamese. They resented Sihanouk's willingness to deal with Communists abroad, and accepted American support for their new regime, called the Khmer Republic. Sihanouk flew to Beijing, China, where he became the head of a government in exile. He curried favor with the Communist opposition in Cambodia as his best chance to return at the head of the government. He called these rebels the Khmer Rouge, or Red Khmer, for their left-leaning politics. The Khmer Rouge were in principle against the monarchy, but they used the popularity of the former Cambodian king to gain legitimacy among ordinary Cambodians.

Meanwhile the Lon Nol regime intensified its campaign to rout the Khmer Rouge. In 1970 South Vietnamese forces with American air cover invaded eastern Cambodia to do what the carpet bombing had not done—clear the area of Viet Minh (North Vietnamese) and Viet Cong (South Vietnamese Communist rebels). The Vietnamese invasion was intended to crush Communist bases in the eastern part of the country and drive the survivors into the forces of Lon Nol, who were waiting in the west to provide the final blow to the retreating Communist forces.

The strategy failed. Lon Nol's repressive measures were resented among ordinary Cambodians nearly as much as the Vietnamese invasion. The result was a surge in support for Cambodia's Communists and a conflict that dragged Cambodia into civil war until 1975, when a strange new brand of communism triumphed under the leadership of the Khmer Rouge.

THE END OF HISTORY

On April 17, 1975, the Khmer Rouge, victorious over Lon Nol's army, entered Phnom Penh. Residents of the capital greeted the jungle fighters with a cautious optimism. They hoped for peace and for a better government than that of Lon Nol's Khmer Republic. The fighters, however, looked like an unlikely group to put the country back on its feet. The urban Cambodians thought the Khmer Rouge fighters looked like mere peasants. In fact, many Khmer Rouge had never seen a city the size of Phnom Penh, but they did not intend to stay in the cities. On the contrary, they intended to make all of Cambodia like their own village hamlets—lands of verdant rice paddies and simple social organization. The Khmer Rouge leaders seized the radio station in Phnom Penh and announced their brave new message: "Two thousand years of Cambodian history have virtually ended,"[9] crackled the message to the startled listeners of the city.

The Khmer Rouge announced that the first year of their reign would be called Year Zero, the beginning of a new Cambodia. The new Cambodia would be a land where all citizens worked together under the watchful eye of the Angkar, the organization. The cities were emptied and residents were stripped of their property and freedom and ordered into the fields. From 1975 to 1979, Cambodia was transformed into a vast labor camp for Cambodia's own citizens. Order was maintained with an almost robotic brutality "Keeping you is not profitable for

 ## THE POISONOUS HILL

Justice under the Khmer Rouge was arbitrary and cruel. The Khmer Rouge never bothered imprisoning people for minor offenses such as theft, civil disobedience, or assault. Perpetrators were simply executed without trial. Prison was reserved for political opponents of Angkar, "the organization" created by the Khmer Rouge to destroy the traditional order of Cambodian life and build upon its ruins a simple agrarian society.

The most famous of the Khmer Rouge prisons was Tuol Sleng, a name that can be translated as "poisonous hill." The prison compound was once a high school, but when the Khmer Rouge took it over, they converted the classrooms into prison cells and interrogation chambers and encircled the compound with electrified barbed wire. Tuol Sleng was also known by the name of S-21, or Security Office 21, the secret police of the Khmer Rouge. Officers of the S-21 used the most grisly methods of interrogation imaginable in their violent attempts to get prisoners to divulge secret plots against the regime. Inmates frequently suffered beatings and torture at the hands of their captors. Today, the Tuol Sleng Museum of Genocidal Crime is a memorial and record of the grim history of the Khmer Rouge regime.

The Khmer Rouge converted many schools into prisons like this one where political dissidents were incarcerated and tortured.

us, discarding you is no loss,"[10] ran one common Khmer Rouge saying. The individual life was dead; there was only the life of the organization.

The new Cambodia, officially called Democratic Kampuchea, cut itself off from the rest of the world and attempted to reverse time by destroying all symbols of modern life. Under the Khmer Rouge, formal education ended. Schools were transformed into prisons where political opponents were tortured. The Khmer Rouge aimed to create a society based on ignorance and obedience. Their method was force. Anyone who opposed the Angkar was either killed on the spot or tortured and then executed. Vietnamese who could not flee fast enough were slaughtered wholesale. Religion was outlawed and especially harsh treatment—usually death—was meted out to the Muslim Cham of Cambodia.

The leaders of Democratic Kampuchea—Pol Pot, Ieng Sary, and Ta Mok, among others—attempted to mimic

China's agrarian revolution, but in half the time. They modeled their economic plan on China's Great Leap Forward and ambitiously called it the Super Great Leap. Cambodia's citizens were driven into the rice paddies to fulfill new quotas for rice production. Those who worked too slowly were whipped or shot. Political indoctrination of weary workers was routine. Class differences were condemned. Cambodian society was to be equal in all respects. In practice, all would be equally miserable. The leaders of the Khmer Rouge, however, enjoyed pleasures that they had not known

POL POT

Among the great villains of history, Pol Pot occupies a unique and infamous place. As Brother Number 1 of the Khmer Rouge, he is responsible for the brutality of Democratic Kampuchea. His policies left one million Cambodians dead, either through starvation, disease, or murder. The killing of one in seven of all Cambodians has been described as autogenocide, the systematic massacre of a people by their own hands.

Pol Pot was born Saloth Sar in 1925. Like many of the original members of the Indochina Communist Party, he was exposed to communism while studying in France. In Paris, he studied electronics on a scholarship and befriended Ieng Sary, who became a leading anticolonial activist and foreign minister under the Khmer Rouge. During his time in power, Pol Pot remained an elusive figure, moving constantly and giving few interviews. After his regime was overthrown, he lived with the remnants of his army in the jungles along the Cambodian border, hunted by various agencies until his death in 1998. With his death, Pol Pot, one of the worst criminals of the twentieth century, eluded justice one final time.

Khmer Rouge leader Pol Pot presided over one of the twentieth century's most brutal regimes.

while hiding in the jungles for so long. In the cities, they drove expensive cars and stole whatever caught their eye.

King Sihanouk, who had returned to Cambodia in 1970, was jailed by the Khmer Rouge, who thanked him for his support by murdering many of his family members. His life was spared, but he remained a prisoner in the strange new Cambodia where neither kings nor prime ministers were welcomed.

THE VIETNAMESE RETURN

The Khmer Rouge discarded not only internal elites but also foreign diplomats and other representatives of normal international relations. Their closest ally was Communist China, which intervened to save the life of Sihanouk. Pol Pot took this advice, but most of the time, the Khmer Rouge leaders listened to no one. Cambodia became one of the most politically isolated countries on earth.

Toward the end of their regime, however, when Khmer Rouge leaders were turning on other Khmer Rouge leaders, the nation burst its boundaries. Khmer Rouge leaders launched murderous raids across the border with Vietnam. These raids unleashed a flood of Vietnamese soldiers who came rushing into Cambodia. The Vietnamese struck from numerous points along the border, driving the Khmer Rouge out of Phnom Penh and into the dense forests of the western part of Cambodia. They then established a new government in Phnom Penh.

The leaders of the Vietnamese-installed government, Hun Sen and Heng Samarin, were ex-Khmer Rouge leaders who fled to Vietnam and gathered other refugees into armed factions. These leaders faced constant guerrilla warfare from the forces of the deposed Khmer Rouge regime. The Americans opposed the Vietnamese-backed Communist government in Phnom Penh, as did the British, the Chinese, and the Thai, who were uncomfortable with Vietnamese influence extending all the way to their border. Once again Cambodia had been reduced to a puppet state pushed and pulled between Thailand on one side and Vietnam on the other.

Cambodian resistance groups, including Sihanouk and his supporters, organized antigovernment forces. The different opposition groups, including the Khmer Rouge, formed armies and often received training from foreign powers. The United States and Great Britain were now in the unsavory position of supporting remnants of the Khmer Rouge. The different factions operated sometimes from Thailand and sometimes from secret bases in Cambodia. This state of civil war lasted from 1979 until the early 1990s.

The government established by the Vietnamese, however, was a great improvement for most Cambodians. They could return to their homes and rebuild their lives. The cities were slowly revived, as Cambodians straggled back from the fields and many returned to their former occupations. Relative stability was restored in many parts of the country, though areas bordering Thailand remained in rebel control. The Vietnamese, due to their own internal problems, withdrew much of their army in 1989. Cambodia was finally left to the Cambodians, who began to pick up the pieces of Cambodian society.

A FRAGILE DEMOCRACY

In 1993, under the glare of international media coverage, nearly 90 percent of all eligible Cambodians went to the polls to choose their government through a peaceful election organized and monitored by the United Nations. The UN had managed to get the major political factions in Cambodia to agree to abide by the outcome of elections that would determine Cambodia's head of state and the makeup of the National Assembly. During the election period, power devolved temporarily to the United Nations Transitional Authority in Cambodia (UNTAC), while a Supreme National Council presided over by Norodom Sihanouk would keep the bellicose parties talking instead of fighting.

The majority of seats in the National Assembly were won by FUNCINPEC, the French acronym for the National United Front for an Independent, Neutral, Peaceful, and Cooperative Cambodia. FUNCINPEC was a coalition of disparate factions that had opposed the Vietnamese-backed government. The party included supporters of Norodom Sihanouk, the Khmer Rouge, and supporters of a previous prime minister, Son Sann. The Cambodian People's Party (CPP), made up of supporters of the Vietnamese-backed government, came in a close second. The smaller Buddhist Liberal Democratic Party (BLDP) came in a distant third. The National Assembly was organized along parliamentary lines, meaning that seats were divided among the parties according to the percentage of votes they won in the general election.

To keep peace between the two main parties, both were allowed a prime minister. FUNCINPEC's Norodom Ranariddh served as first prime minister and Hun Sen of the CPP served as second prime minister. The prime ministers would manage the day-to-day affairs of the country and try to keep their supporters from going back to war. According to the new constitution of Cambodia, the head of state would be the constitutional monarch Norodom Sihanouk. The king, who had started as a powerless figurehead, was now called upon once again to play the role of a unifying symbol of Cambodia, while the governing would be left to elected ministers. The king still plays a role in the political life of the country, but by and large he appears to be content playing the ceremonial monarch. He often visits the royal residence in Siem Reap, a short distance from where the god-kings ruled Cambodia from Angkor.

Prince Ranariddh (left) and Hun Sen confer prior to being sworn in as joint prime ministers. The two agreed to share power in the aftermath of Cambodia's civil war.

The relationship between the two prime ministers has not been so cordial. Some might say that taking the extraordinary step of having two prime ministers ensured conflict between them. In July 1997, Hun Sen ousted Norodom Ranariddh, taking for himself the position of sole prime minister. The coup was a reminder of how volatile the political situation is in Cambodia. Since then Hun Sen has ruled as Cambodia's strongman, intimidating political opponents and curbing public criticism when possible.

In July 1998, Hun Sen called a general election, marked by political intrigue and outright intimidation. Phnom Penh was on edge as supporters of various factions prowled the streets, often clashing with opposing factions. Hun Sen was elected prime minister, the position he had already taken for himself by force. Despite international criticism of Hun Sen's tactics, the Cambodian prime minister has generally upheld the constitution. Sihanouk still serves as king and the elected members of the National Assembly still make the laws of Cambodia, subject to Hun Sen's approval.

6

Cambodia Today

Cambodia today is a nation struggling to modernize. It has a representative government and tentative political stability. In light of the modern history of Cambodia, one might imagine a country in ruins, depopulated by the murderous Khmer Rouge and years of civil war. In fact, Cambodia is a country humming with life. Cities such as Phnom Penh and Battambang, though not as populous as other Asian cities, are beehives of activity. Motor scooters weave through the crowds and throngs of people shop for daily necessities—fruits, vegetables, rice, clothing, cooking utensils—much of which can be bought from street vendors or at outdoor markets. Shops selling the latest electronic goods also line the streets.

Along quieter lanes and in villages, monks wear their saffron-colored robes, draped over one shoulder as they have been worn for centuries. Soldiers in olive-drab uniforms and sandals mill around archaeological sites as security guards. The military provides a small but stable wage in a country with high unemployment. The military and the Buddhist orders provide two career options for young Cambodian men. It is not unusual, in fact, to encounter Cambodians who have been both a monk and a soldier. As in neighboring Thailand, Cambodian men can enter a Buddhist monastery for brief periods, which are viewed as periods of atonement and are believed to bring fortune to the family.

Life in the countryside has the same rhythm as it has for centuries. Rice is still planted and harvested by hand. The cloth *krama*, or turban, provides shade from the sun. Women often work side by side with men and even the children are called upon to help bring in the crops at harvest time. Education today is compulsory for children, but, especially in the countryside, school attendance is not enforced.

EDUCATION

Until the arrival of the French, education in Cambodia was usually provided by the *wats*, or Buddhist temples, where young men learned to read and memorize religious texts. Buddhism was naturally the primary subject taught in the wats, but sometimes Cambodian history and the Khmer language were included. Since only boys received training from the monks, relying on the wats for education resulted in very low literacy levels for Cambodian girls and women.

Under the French, Western educational methods were introduced into Cambodia. The French established schools, mainly in larger towns, with classes taught in French, and mastery of the colonial language was seen as a way to improve one's lot in the French colony. French is preserved today as the second major language aside from Khmer, though English is rapidly gaining ground. The survival of French is partly due to the fondness of the royal family for using French. Cambodian royals and other members of the upper classes often sent their children to study in France. Norodom Sihanouk, for example, attended a military academy in France, where he learned French cavalry techniques from the French officer corps.

THE FLAVORS OF CAMBODIA

Famine in Cambodia has always been the result of political turmoil. Normally, Cambodia is blessed with fertile land suitable for the cultivation of rice, while fruits grow abundantly and in great variety, and fish and prawns can be easily plucked from Cambodia's many waterways.

The abundance and variety of food in Cambodia has given rise to a unique cuisine. Most dishes are served with rice, which is stickier than varieties usually served in the West. Vegetables are generally served with the rice as well as chicken, duck, pork, prawns, or fish. The food is seasoned, but more mildly than in neighboring Thailand. Adventurous eaters can try fried spiders, locusts, or snake meat. Food stalls line the streets in many cities and towns, and fresh fruit juices, sugarcane juice, and Cambodian beer, including the popular Angkor brand, are sold to the thirsty. Cambodia's long history of contact with the Thai and Vietnamese has given diversity to the cuisine of Cambodia. The Chinese also serve their native dishes in restaurants throughout Cambodia.

CAMBODIA'S ROYAL MATINEE IDOL

Norodom Sihanouk's sense of theater is legendary. He was the great actor of modern Cambodian politics and his country was his stage. But unable to resist the glamor of the silver screen, Sihanouk launched himself as both director and actor. Between 1966 and 1969, the former king of Cambodia directed nine feature films, usually with himself in a lead role.

For Sihanouk, the cinema was one more way to enhance his own stature and publicize the Cambodia that he loved, a land of natural wonders and heroic people. Sihanouk realized that the cinema was an effective way of influencing a mass audience, and no effort was spared to make his movies. He employed government ministers and royal family members as actors and extras and called in Cambodia's armed forces when he wanted to shoot a battle scene. Sihanouk hoped that Cambodia's film industry would bring recognition to Cambodia. To attract international attention, Sihanouk held the Phnom Penh International Film Festival in 1968 and 1969, winning prizes in both events. The following year, he was driven into exile.

Although the French can be credited with introducing modern educational standards to Cambodia and influencing a generation of well-off Cambodians to study in France, they were never very interested in establishing a widespread educational system in Cambodia. The French administrators considered Cambodia to be a buffer for the principal Indochinese colony of Vietnam. The French were much more involved in the direct governing of the Vietnamese than they were of the Cambodians. Many French scholars and missionaries took a passionate interest in establishing educational institutions in Cambodia, but their efforts never reached the majority of Cambodians.

The true triumph of the French educational system in Cambodia arrived only after the French had departed. King Sihanouk, the former puppet of the French government, proved to be a vigorous advocate of education in Cambodia. In the years after the French departed, the number of public schools more than doubled under Sihanouk's guidance. He established compulsory education and raised enrollment to unprecedented levels. Sihanouk also founded universities, hoping to produce world-class engineers, lawyers, doctors, and other professionals who would help build a modern and prosperous Cambodia. These educational reforms succeeded so well that by the 1960s Cambodia had more educated students than it had jobs for them to fill. The economy had not kept pace and political instability dampened future prospects for college graduates.

Under the Khmer Rouge education ceased entirely. It was not only frowned on but outlawed. Teachers were murdered, and schools were appropriated by the Khmer Rouge for prisons and other facilities or simply abandoned. The Khmer Rouge so persecuted the educated that people were murdered for wearing glasses—-thought to be a sign of an educated person—and for speaking foreign languages. The consequences for Cambodia were dramatic. The Khmer Rouge largely succeeded in producing an uneducated population.

Many in modern Cambodia today were educated during the Vietnamese-backed People's Republic of Kampuchea, which ruled from 1979 to 1989. Hun Sen, who headed the government, attempted to rebuild Cambodia's educational system. Nearly everything in Cambodia at that time was infused

Prime Minister Hun Sen addresses the French media. Sen infused Cambodia's educational system with Communist ideology.

with political ideology. Because the Vietnamese backed Hun Sen's government, Communist ideology was stressed in the school system. The Soviet Union, a backer of Communist Vietnam, considered the Hun Sen government a good opportunity to spread its ideology. The Soviets, therefore, sent technical and monetary aid to Cambodia and even teachers for the schools. The Soviets placed a special emphasis on agricultural technologies and sciences and mathematics that would foster industrial development. At the university level, classes were sometimes taught in Russian. Many Cambodians benefited from the Soviet teachers, though their studies usually had an ideological slant.

Since the elections of 1993, Cambodia has benefited from large infusions of aid from foreign governments, the United Nations, and nongovernmental organizations. Much of the money has been earmarked for education, and today, Cambodia's illiteracy rate is dropping. Schools are being established even in remote villages. In the cities, attending university has become a common goal among the young, and many private schools have opened to teach business skills for the modern economy. English-language schools have become more popular than French-language schools and computer classes are perhaps the most highly sought after of all.

TEACHING OF ELDERS

If education represented to the Khmer Rouge a corrupting, Western decadence, religion was viewed as an evil superstition. In Democratic Kampuchea, wats were destroyed or desecrated, monks were slaughtered or forced to work alongside other Cambodians. Some of the Khmer Rouge leaders, however, consoled their own parents by letting them visit wats staffed by a few monks.

Despite their best efforts, Buddhism survived the Khmer Rouge atrocities intact. Today more than 90 percent of all Cambodians are Theravada Buddhists. Theravada Buddhism is also known as the Teaching of the Elders. It represents one of the two great branches of Buddhism that spread from India into East Asia. The other branch is sometimes called the northern branch, since it traveled northward from India to Nepal, Tibet, and onward into China, Korea, and Japan. The northern branch of East Asian Buddhism is generally referred to as Mahayana, or "Great Wheel," Buddhism. Mahayana Buddhists refer to Theravada Buddhism as Hinayana, or "Lesser Wheel," Buddhism. Theravada Buddhists prefer the term Theravada, since they consider the wheel distinction as belittling their own sect. Theravada spread from India along the southern coast of Asia, both by land and by sea, and is therefore also known as the southern branch.

Theravada Buddhism emphasizes the four truths taught by the Buddha, namely that life is suffering, that suffering is caused by desire, that eliminating desire will end suffering, and that the middle way is the path to eliminating desire and therefore suffering. In other words, suffering is caused by human desire for money, sex, power, and all the other things that motivate the average person. To rid oneself of the suffering caused by mortal desires, one must follow a path of moderation. To follow the middle way is to avoid extremes, but not to give up all worldly ambitions. It is something of a balancing act.

Two Theravada Buddhist monks pose for a photo. Theravada monks abstain from earthly pleasures and spend much of their time meditating.

The lives of Buddhist monks are more austere than those of average Buddhists. Monks abstain from marriage and sexual relations, perform selfless acts, and spend much time meditating. Generally speaking Theravada Buddhism is a moderate religion that places much emphasis on humility, personal introspection, and the regulation of one's own behavior. In the wake of the Khmer Rouge atrocities, Buddhism seemed to grow stronger in Cambodia, perhaps as a source of strength in a time of great suffering.

The Buddhist emphasis on moderation and self-improvement makes Cambodians, in general, a restrained people. They tend to be a modest people, not inclined to trumpet their own successes or flaunt their wealth. In contrast to the restraint of Theravada Buddhism, Mahayana Buddhists have a much more expansive set of rituals, hence the name Greater Wheel Buddhism. Mahayana Buddhism arose from the attempts to fit Buddhism into new cultures. In China, for example, Buddhism had to compete with the prevailing attitudes of Confucianism and the pantheon of Taoist gods. The result was a blending of the religions into a much less austere form of Buddhism.

Mahayana Buddhism is practiced among the Chinese community in Cambodia. It is not unusual for a Chinese Cambodian to honor the birthday of Confucius with religious rites such as the burning of incense, while at other times of the year honoring both Taoist gods and the Buddha. The Chinese, in general, also place less value on austerity, and have specific gods to whom they pray to increase their worldly fortunes.

ISLAM

It is an extraordinary fact that there are more Muslims in Southeast Asia than in all of the Middle East, where Islam first arose in the seventh century A.D. The majority of those Muslims live in Indonesia and Malaysia, where Islam is the predominant religion. In Cambodia, Islam is practiced by a small minority. It is the religion of the Cham, and it has been largely confined to their community.

It has been argued that Islam spread rapidly in the Far East because it offered a clearly defined set of principles to replace the hodepodge of local religions and animist beliefs. Islam is a monotheistic religion; with the sole God being called Allah in the Arabic of the holy book of Islam, the Koran. Islam offers believers a series of religious requirements by which to order their days and give purpose to life. A Muslim, for example, is required to pray five times a day facing Islam's most holy city, Mecca, located in the western part of Saudi Arabia. The *muezzin*—the public crier of a mosque—calls the faithful to pray in mosques in Cambodia or sometimes uses a drum. If it is not convenient to attend a mosque, then prayers can be performed wherever the devotee is.

CAODAISM

Of all the minority religions in Cambodia one of the most unusual is Caodaism. Just as Buddhism arose from contacts with Thailand to Cambodia's west, Caodaism is an import from Cambodia's eastern neighbor, Vietnam. Caodaism is the third major religion of Vietnam, after Buddhism and Roman Catholicism. The name Cao Dai refers to the high altar, thought to be the home of the supreme god, sometimes called the Cae Dai. Caodaism incorporates beliefs of Buddhism, Taoism, Christianity, Confucianism, and Geniism, which is a folk religion of Vietnam.

The religion was founded by a Vietnamese civil servant in Cochin China, a French administrative unit of Vietnam, corresponding to the southern part of the country. In 1926, a band of followers of the Cao Dai organized the religion and elected its first pope. Caodaists have an elaborate organization of church officials that resembles the Roman Catholic hierarchy. Their altars are decorated with a representation of God as an all-seeing, divine eye. But they also worship Buddha, Lao Tse (the founder of Taoism), Jesus, Confucius, and Khuong Thai Cong (to represent Geniism). Caodaists also recognize three saints: Sun Yat-sen, the revolutionary leader of modern China; the French novelist Victor Hugo; and Trang Trinh, a Vietnamese poet. They also celebrate great modern figures such as Mahatma Gandhi and Winston Churchill.

Caodaism is a fascinating example of a modern religion that attempts to assimilate aspects of many, often competing, faiths. Its followers in Cambodia are limited to a few thousand, but it is an interesting legacy of Cambodia's long contact with Vietnam.

A Cao Dai devotee prostrates himself beneath the watchful eye of the supreme being.

Generally, a prayer mat, sometimes a beautifully woven rug, will be unfurled for the Muslim to perform his prayers facing Mecca. He is required to pray on his knees and bend in the direction of Mecca. Cambodian Muslims also strive to

The sun sets behind the dome and minarets of a Cambodian mosque. The Cham people comprise the majority of Cambodia's Muslims.

make the pilgrimage to Mecca if they have adequate funds. The pilgrimage, or *hajj*, is one of the five pillars, or sacred beliefs and obligations, of Islam. A Muslim who has made the pilgrimage to Mecca has the right to affix the honorific Hajji to the front of his name, indicating that he is one who has made the pilgrimage. Another pillar is the giving of alms, which Muslims do in many ways and with the belief that donating money is a sacred duty.

Islam in Cambodia is perhaps most notable for its relaxed attitude. Cham Muslims find certain symbolic acts to be a worthy expression of their faith. Fasting during the month of Ramadan on the lunar calendar is often performed only one day a week. Just as Buddhists and Christians have organized into different sects with variations in belief and in practice, the Cham have developed a unique form of Islam that is easily identifiable as Islam but which has some particularly Cambodian aspects.

ARTS AND CULTURE

Many Cambodians today are determined to salvage the traditional arts of Cambodia, which were nearly extinguished during the rule of the Khmer Rouge. Many practitioners of Cambodia's traditional arts, including dance, music, and painting, were singled out by the Khmer Rouge for execution; many more starved to death or succumbed to disease.

Today the government, with generous international support, has insured that facilities are available to teach the Cambodian people traditional arts. Much optimism is focused on the School of Fine Arts in Phnom Penh, which opened its doors in 1981 with just a few teachers. The school has blossomed since then, and offers classes on the arts from

 ## THE SOUNDS OF CAMBODIA

Like most Asian countries, Cambodia has a lively modern music scene. It is a mix of native Khmer pop music and imported sounds from around the world. Although the music industry suffered along with other arts and entertainments under the Khmer Rouge, it slowly reemerged in the years after 1975. Today, a domestic music industry promotes pop singers in Khmer. Khmer musicians have had a lively relationship with overseas Cambodian communities. The Cambodian emigrants, influenced by the music in their adopted countries, introduced new sounds and recording technology to Cambodia. Cantonese, Japanese, and English-language music is also popular in Cambodia. Cambodians have also caught the karaoke bug, which began in Japan and spread throughout Asia. In Cambodia, karaoke parlors are a common meeting place for teenagers, who can sing along with their favorite pop stars.

Traditional music in Cambodia has survived the competition with pop music. Instruments such as the tro khmae (three-stringed fiddle), khsae muoy (single-stringed bowed instrument), and the roneat (a xylophone), are a fixture at weddings, during religious festivals, and other cultural celebrations. Some of the traditional instruments still played today in Cambodia resemble instruments carved into bas-relief on the temples of the Angkorean age.

traditional dance and music to piano, ballet, and modern sculpture.

Perhaps the most famous of all the traditional arts of Cambodia was Cambodia's classical ballet, or court dancing. The ballet was traditionally performed only by women, dressed in elaborate and brilliantly colored costumes topped by temple-shaped hats. The performance combined rhythmic music and elegant movements and often retold the stories of the Hindu epic *Ramayana*. The stories of the Hindu epic have become something of a national mythology in Cambodia. "The beauty of these dances against the dark mystery of the temple," recorded the English author W. Somerset Maugham at a performance staged at Angkor, "made it the most beautiful and unearthly sight imaginable."[11] So important was the Royal Ballet as a symbol of Cambodia's past that great efforts have been made to preserve it, and teaching traditional dance is one of the main functions of the School of Fine Arts.

Another art that is being revived is the art of shadow puppets. Shadow puppets are intricately crafted representations of human or divine figures, made from cow or buffalo hide. They "perform" behind a screen illuminated by a light. The light casts the puppets in lively shapes on the screen. Actors narrate the the play, giving a voice to the puppets, while the puppeteers manipulate the puppets from behind the screen. This art, called *nang sbaek thom* in Khmer, is also practiced in Thailand, Malaysia, and Indonesia. The subjects of the shadow plays are sometimes drawn from Hindu mythology, a rich tradition of local Cambodian folklore and history provides additional sources.

Preserving and celebrating Cambodian culture has a certain momentum in Cambodia today. Years of hardship and deprivation have created a yearning for entertainments and the desire to celebrate the positive sides of Cambodian history. There is much competition, however, from foreign arts and entertainments, especially in Cambodia's urban centers. Cambodian teenagers, like teenagers all over Asia, sing along to their favorite music in karaoke clubs. Some of the music is native Khmer, but much is imported from Japan, Hong Kong, and the West. Cambodian cinema, which received such a boost from the patronage of King Sihanouk, is still turning out Khmer-language films.

These films, however, face tough competition from the imported films for Cambodian audiences. Cambodia has reentered the world stage; no longer is it a country at war and cut off from the outside world.

EPILOGUE
SOME UNSOLVED PROBLEMS

As Cambodia struggles to take its place in the community of modern nations, it must confront the painful legacy of Cambodian history. The country is one of the poorest in Southeast Asia. Its economic hardship stems partly from the years of Khmer Rouge rule. Deciding how to respond to the legacy of the Khmer Rouge is proving to be one of the most difficult problems for Cambodia to face.

MOSTLY THE OLD WAY

After wreaking havoc on the economy of Thailand and other nations in Asia, the Asian economic crisis of 1997, for the most part, did not affect Cambodia. There was simply not much in the way of financial infrastructure to destroy in Cambodia. The economic crisis generally affected banking and currencies, financial markets and investment. Cambodia is still just developing the infrastructure of a modern economy.

The traditional economy, however, reestablished itself with great success in the 1980s and 1990s. The starvation caused by the export of rice to China and North Korea under the Khmer Rouge had come to an end, and so too had the failed reforms in agriculture. Farmers returned to the old ways, and Cambodia regained its reputation for being a land rich in foodstuffs. The rice that is exported today brings in profits for Cambodian exporters and leaves no one hungry. Agriculture, for example, accounted for 90 percent of Cambodia's gross domestic product in 1985 and employed 80 percent of the workforce. Other major crops include corn, sesame seeds, and soybeans. Rubber plantations provide another major cash crop for Cambodia and a valuable source of foreign exchange. Rubber is sold abroad and the foreign revenues help stabilize the economy of Cambodia.

Industry in Cambodia is still developing. Among the more important industries are textiles and tobacco processing.

Cambodia also has many small manufacturers, sometimes no more than a family or a group of families. These small manufacturers are subcontractors of larger manufacturers. In the textile industry, for example, a family-run garment shop might produce so many pieces per day for a larger company, which hires many such small manufacturers to fill its orders.

Despite Cambodia's recent economic gains, a persistent problem is corruption. The problem is deeply embedded in the factional politics of Cambodia and extends throughout the economy. Bribes, kickbacks, intimidation, skimming profits, and a weak judicial system to enforce the laws scares off foreign investment and hurts the domestic economy. The problem is tied to the unstable political situation of modern Cambodia, where Cambodians are still working toward the establishment of a stable government and coming to grips with their past.

GHOSTS OF THE PAST

During the 1990s, when Cambodia's political leaders were scrambling for electoral support, a grim exercise in pragmatism took place. Members of the Khmer Rouge, still hiding out in their jungle bases

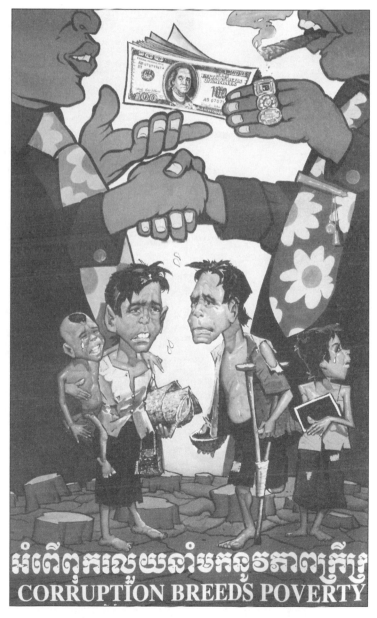

A Cambodian public awareness poster illustrates the injustice of corruption. Corruption runs rampant in nearly every sector of Cambodian society.

អំពើពុករលួយនាំមកនូវភាពក្រីក្រ

CORRUPTION BREEDS POVERTY

along the border with Thailand, became the subject of an intense public relations competition. Politicians offered Khmer Rouge soldiers amnesty if they would come out of the jungle. Some army commanders were told that they could retain command of their troops, if they would only dress in government uniforms.

The Khmer Rouge had set up a small fiefdom along Thailand's border. They had developed a small local economy, selling wood products, precious stones, and other goods to Thais across the border. Their leaders, however, had begun to squabble among themselves. Their ideological fervor had fizzled and their followers were little more than well-armed smugglers. Many wanted to take the government offer for amnesty.

In August 1996, Pol Pot denounced his old comrade Ieng Sary, the Khmer Rouge foreign minister during their rule and number-three man in the organization. Ieng Sary responded by defecting to the government with a large swath of Khmer Rouge soldiers. Pol Pot next turned on Son Sen, the former defense minister. It was his last gasp of persecution, and self-annihilation. The Khmer Rouge had finally turned on its own leaders. Ta Mok, perhaps the Khmer Rouge's most feared military commander, arrested Pol Pot and placed him on trial. In 1998 Pol Pot died from unknown causes. The Khmer Rouge was effectively finished; most members made some arrangement with the government or just faded into local life.

The legacy of the Khmer Rouge, on the other hand, continues to haunt Cambodia. Calls for a UN war crimes trial have so far been rejected by the Cambodian government. There has been talk of trying the Khmer Rouge in Cambodian courts, but no prosecutions have materialized. Cambodians are just beginning to openly discuss the horrors of the past. The crimes of Cambodia's painful modern history are still being documented. But perhaps most troubling are the backgrounds of Cambodia's present politicians. Hun Sen and other major politicians were once part of the Khmer Rouge. Although they later defected, what might be uncovered about their role in the Khmer Rouge? Even King Sihanouk was at one time allied with the Khmer Rouge. His stature in fact drew many converts to their cause.

   Accounting for Cambodia's past could take years, even
decades. For now, Cambodia is at peace, and Cambodians
are rebuilding a once-great nation. Even as Phnom Penh,
Battambang, Sihanoukville, and the other towns and cities of
Cambodia struggle to modernize, Angkor rises from the
Cambodian countryside as a lasting reminder of the re-
sourcefulness of Cambodia's people.

FACTS ABOUT CAMBODIA

GOVERNMENT

Official name: Kingdom of Cambodia (Preahreacheanachakr Kampuchea)

Capital: Phnom Penh

Form of government: From September 1993, multiparty democracy under a constitutional monarchy

Official language: Khmer (spoken by 95% of Cambodians); French and English are the major secondary languages

Chief administrative units:

Provinces: Banteay Mean Cheay, Batdambang, Kampong Cham, Kampong Chhnang, Kampong Spoe, Kampong Thum, Kampot, Kandal, Kaoh Kong, Kracheh, Mondol Kiri, Otdar Mean Cheay, Pouthisat, Preah Vihear, Prey Veng, Rotanah Kiri, Siem Reab, Stoeng Treng, Svay Rieng, Takev

Municipalities: Keb, Pailin, Phnom Pehn, Preah Seihanu

PEOPLE

(Note: all estimates are 2001 figures unless otherwise indicated)

Total population: 12,491,500

Population distribution:

0–14 years: 41.25%

15–64 years: 55.28%

65 years and over: 3.47%

Population growth rate: 2.25%

Birth rate: 33.16 births/1,000 population

Death rate: 10.65 deaths/1,000 population

Life expectancy at birth:

total population: 56.82

males: 54.62

females: 59.12

Ethnic groups: Khmer 90%, Vietnamese 5%, Chinese 1%, other 4%

Religions: Theravada Buddhist 95%, other 5%

Literacy rate: 35%

Official holidays:

> January 1 New Year's Day
>
> March 8 Women's Day
>
> April 13 Khmer New Year
>
> May 1 Labor Day
>
> June 1 International Children's Day
>
> September 24 Constitution Day
>
> October 23 Paris Peace Agreement
>
> October 30 King's Birthday
>
> November 9 Independence Day
>
> December 10 UN Human Rights Day

Major festivals:

> Lunar New Year: late January to early February (celebrated mainly by Chinese and Vietnamese minorities)
>
> Khmer New Year: mid-April (celebrated for three days)
>
> Chap Preah Nengkal (Royal Ploughing Festival): early May
>
> Bom Om Tuk (celebration of the end of the wet season): early November

LAND

Area:

> total: 181,040 sq km (69,901 sq mi)
>
> land: 176,520 sq km (65,156 sq mi)
>
> water: 4,520 sq km (1,745 sq mi)

Bordering countries: Thailand, Vietnam, Laos

Bordering body of water: Gulf of Thailand

Land boundaries: 2,572 km (993 sq mi)

Longest river: Mekong River

Coastline: 443 km (275 mi)

Largest lake: Tonle Sap

Lowest point of elevation: Gulf of Thailand 0 m (0 ft)

Highest point of elevation: Phnom Aoral 1,810 m (5,938 ft)

CLIMATE

Average temps: 70–95°F (21–35°C)

Hottest month: April, when temperatures can reach 105°F (40°C)

Cambodia's climate is largely defined by two monsoon seasons: the cooler, drier northeastern monsoon from November to February and the warmer, wetter southwestern monsoon from May to October.

ECONOMY

Official currency: riel (KHR)

Gross domestic product: (GDP) 3 billion (2000)

Major industries: tourism, rice milling, fishing, wood and wood products, rubber, cement, gem mining, textiles and garment assembly

Major agricultural products: rice, rubber, corn, vegetables

Export commodities: timber, garments, rubber, rice, fish

GDP by sector (1998):

agriculture 43%

industry 20%

services 37%

Population below the poverty line: 36% (1997 estimate)

Unemployment rate: 2.8% (1999 estimate)

Export partners (countries that admit Cambodian exports): Vietnam 18%, Thailand 15%, United States 10%, Singapore 8%, China 5% (1997)

Import partners (countries from which Cambodia imports products): Thailand 16%, Vietnam 9%, Japan 7%, Hong Kong 5%, China 5% (1997)

NOTES

CHAPTER 1: THE LAND

1. Quoted in Thierry Zephir, *Khmer: Lost Empire of Cambodia.* New York: Abrams, 1998, p. 108.

CHAPTER 2: THE KHMER AND THEIR COMPATRIOTS

2. Quoted in Zephir, *Khmer*, p. 103.

CHAPTER 3: THE RISE AND FALL OF ANGKOR

3. Quoted in David P. Chandler, *The Land and People of Cambodia.* New York: HarperCollins, 1991, p. 104.
4. Quoted in Chandler, *The Land and People of Cambodia*, p. 105.
5. Quoted in Zephir, *Khmer*, p. 44.
6. Quoted in Zephir, *Khmer*, pp. 108–109.

CHAPTER 4: THE ROAD TO INDEPENDENCE

7. Quoted in Chandler, *The Land and People of Cambodia*, p. 97.

CHAPTER 5: STRUGGLE FOR SURVIVAL

8. Quoted in Claire Griffiths, *Insight Guide: Laos and Cambodia.* Singapore: APA Publications, 2000, p. 196.
9. Quoted in Arnold R. Isaacs et al., *Pawns of War: Cambodia and Laos.* The Vietnam Experience series. Boston: Boston Publishing, 1987, p. 116.
10. Quoted in Chandler, *Land and People of Cambodia*, p. 149.

CHAPTER 6: CAMBODIA TODAY

11. Quoted in Griffiths, *The Insight Guide*, p. 226.

CHRONOLOGY

B.C.

ca. 5000
Cave-dwelling people first appear in northwestern Cambodia.

ca. 2000
Early Cambodians begin casting bronze.

ca. 600–400
Knowledge of ironworking spreads across Southeast Asia.

A.D.

ca. 400
Evidence of Khmer and Sanskrit inscriptions carved in stone.

802
Dynasty of King Jayavarman II begins in northwestern Cambodia.

802–1431
Angkor civilization.

ca. 1130
King Suryavarman II orders the building of Angkor Wat.

1178–1220
Reign of Jayavarman VII.

1296
Visit of Chinese official Zhou Daguan to Angkor.

1430
Thai invade Angkor.

1794

Thai choose new monarch for Cambodians, initiating a period of Thai-Vietnamese struggle for control of Cambodia.

1841

Cambodian officials revolt against Vietnamese rulers; Thai re-invade Cambodia.

1858

King Duang unsuccessfully seeks French protection for Cambodia.

1863

France proclaims protectorate of Cambodia.

1884–1886

Uprising against French rule; Sisowath, brother of King Norodom, aids French in quelling the rebellion.

1904

With French backing, Sisowath becomes king of Cambodia.

1927

Sisowath is succeeded by his son, Monivong.

1941

Japanese occupy Cambodia; Monivong dies; Norodom Sihanouk, grandson of Monivong, is crowned king of Cambodia.

1945

Japanese declare independence for Cambodia; Japanese defeat ends World War II; French reoccupy Cambodia.

1946–1953

Cambodians resist French occupation.

1953

French protectorate of Cambodia ends; Cambodia proclaims its independence November 9.

1955

Sihanouk abdicates, forms new political party, the Sangkum, that wins control of the reestablished National Assembly; Sihanouk becomes prime minister.

1960
Founding of Cambodian Communist Party.

1963
Sihanouk breaks off economic relations with the United States; Pol Pot becomes head of Cambodian Communist Party.

1967
Anti-Sihanouk Communist insurgency begins.

1969
United States bombs Vietnamese supply lines in Cambodia with approval of Sihanouk.

1970
Sihanouk is overthrown; Lon Nol seizes power.

1975
Communists capture Phnom Penh and take control of Cambodia, emptying cities and launching all-encompassing agrarian social experiment; Pol Pot renames Cambodia as Democratic Kampuchea.

1979
Vietnamese army invades Cambodia, toppling Pol Pot and installing a Communist government friendly to Vietnam; Pol Pot and other Khmer Rouge leaders flee to Thailand.

1981
Pol Pot, Sihanouk, Son Sann form coalition government in exile that is recognized by the United Nations.

1989
Vietnamese forces withdraw from Cambodia.

1991
Prince Sihanouk returns to Cambodia.

1993
United Nations supervises general elections, which result in a coalition government of Prince Norodom Ranariddh's FUNCINPEC Party and Hun Sen's People's Party.

1996

Some Khmer Rouge leaders defect to the government in return for amnesty.

1997

Pol Pot placed under house arrest.

1998

Pol Pot dies; remnants of Khmer Rouge disband.

FOR FURTHER READING

BOOKS

Clive J. Christie, *Southeast Asia in the Twentieth Century: A Reader.* New York: Tauris, 1998. A collection of essays on the political landscape of Southeast Asia.

Chanrithy Him, *When Broken Glass Floats: Growing Up Under the Khmer Rouge.* New York: W.W. Norton, 2000. A first-person narrative of growing up during the Khmer Rouge reign of terror.

Milton Osborne, *Sihanouk: Prince of Light, Prince of Darkness.* Sydney, Australia: Allen and Unwin, 1994. A biography of the man who was at various times king, president, and exile, and who has played a major part in shaping Cambodia's history in recent decades.

Loung Ung, *First They Killed My Father: A Daughter of Cambodia Remembers.* New York: HarperCollins, 2000. A tale of surviving the mad reign of Pol Pot by the national spokesperson for the Campaign for a Landmine Free World.

WEBSITES

Cambodia Information Center (www.cambodia.org). A nonprofit organization that provides various information on Cambodia, with links to other resources.

embassy.org (www.embassy.org/cambodia). The official site of The Royal Cambodian Embassy in Washington, D.C.

Central Intelligence Agency (www.cia.gov/cia). Facts, statistics, and maps of Cambodia, courtesy of the Central Intelligence Agency.

Phnom Penh Post (www.phnompenhpost.com). Online version of a national, daily, English-language newspaper published in the Cambodia capital.

Angkor Wat (www.angkorwat.org). Information about the world's largest religious complex, including photos, facts and figures, and travel information.

WORKS CONSULTED

David P. Chandler, *A History of Cambodia.* Boulder, CO: West-view Press, 1992. A basic primer for serious students of Cambodian history.

———, *The Land and People of Cambodia.* New York: HarperCollins, 1991. A good overview of Cambodia by a scholar of Cambodian civilizaton and director of Southeast Asian Studies at Monash University in Melbourne, Australia.

———, *The Tragedy of Cambodian History: Politics, War, and Revolution Since 1945.* New Haven, CT: Yale University Press, 1991. Chandler looks at the array of disasters and upheavals that have shaped the modern Cambodian state.

Joan D. Criddle and Teeda Butt Mam, *To Destroy You Is No Loss: The Odyssey of a Cambodian Family.* New York: Atlantic Monthly Press, 1987. The tale of a Phnom Penh family that was driven out of the city and into forced labor in the countryside during the rule of the Khmer Rouge.

Claire Griffiths, *Insight Guide: Laos and Cambodia.* Singapore: APA Publications, 2000. A travel guide to Laos and Cambodia full of interesting facts, dates, and vivid descriptions of numerous places.

Mary Somers Heidhues, *Southeast Asia: A Concise History.* New York: Thames & Hudson, 2000. An insightful introduction to Southeast Asian history from the earliest times to the end of colonialism and the formation of modern Southeast Asia.

Arnold R. Isaacs et al., *Pawns of War: Cambodia and Laos.* The Vietnam Experience series. Boston: Boston Publishing, 1987. A look at the effects of the Vietnam War on the neighboring countries of Cambodia and Laos; includes many pictures of wartime Cambodia.

Henry Kamm, *Cambodia: Report from a Stricken Land.* New York: Arcade, 1998. A *New York Times* Southeast Asia correspondent's anecdotal history of Cambodia from the early 1970s to the late 1990s, based on his three decades as a reporter in the region.

Nick Ray, *Cambodia.* Hawthorn, Australia: Lonely Planet, 2000. An excellent guidebook to Cambodia with much useful information.

Russell R. Ross., ed., *Cambodia: A Country Study.* Area Handbook series. Washington, DC: U.S. Government Printing Office, 1990. An excellent if somewhat technical gazetteer of Cambodia by the Federal Research Division of the Library of Congress.

Robert Shawcross, *Cambodia's New Deal.* Washington, DC: Carnegie Endowment for International Peace, 1994. A brief survey of the problems, from political instability to land mines, that Cambodia faces today.

Thierry Zephir, *Khmer: The Lost Empire of Cambodia.* New York: Abrams, 1998. An introduction to the medieval civilization of the Khmer people with many beautiful illustrations and photographs of Angkor Wat, Angkor Thom, and other Khmer architectural wonders.

INDEX

Picture Credits

ABOUT THE AUTHOR

Robert Green is the senior editor of the *Taipei Review,* a monthly publication of the Government Information Office of the Republic of China. He holds a master's degree in journalism from New York University and a bachelor's degree in English literature from Boston University. He first traveled to Taiwan on a Blakemore Foundation Language Grant. Among his twenty-five books are two other titles in the Modern Nations series, *China* and *Taiwan.*